In defence of Britis

In defence of British openness

Evidence and ideas on how we might think about a multiracial country

Richard Norrie

CIVITAS

First published
February 2022

55 Tufton Street
London SW1P 3QL

email: books@civitas.org.uk

ISBN 978-1-912581-28-3

Independence: Civitas: Institute for the Study of Civil Society is a registered educational charity (No. 1085494) and a company limited by guarantee (No. 04023541). Civitas is financed from a variety of private sources to avoid over-reliance on any single or small group of donors.

All the Institute's publications seek to further its objective of promoting the advancement of learning. The views expressed are those of the authors, not of the Institute.

Typeset by Typetechnique

Printed in Great Britain
by 4edge Limited, Essex

Contents

Author

Richard Norrie is Director of the Statistics and Policy Research Programme at Civitas.

Summary

- This report is a defence of British institutions against radical and unspecified demands that necessitate their destruction. It is argued that they benefit us all and need to be nurtured and even repaired, and this responsibility falls on those of all ethnicities, majority and minority alike.
- The idea is to provide a different way to think about race that sees people of an ethnic minority as inheritors and custodians of the British way of life as much as anyone else, sharing responsibility for its defence and upkeep.
- What came to be known as the Sewell report, published in April 2021, found that whatever statistical differences there were between ethnic or racial groups, they more often than not had little to do with either race or racism.
- This conclusion provoked 'fire and fury' among sections of the commentariat, politicians, and also the general public.
- This report examines the fallout from the affair, scrutinising both the report itself and its critics.
- It is concluded that the critics were usually wide off the mark, often resorting to critiques that the report 'denied the lived-experience', without any objective basis on which this claim could be measured or judged.

- That is not to say the Sewell report can escape criticism; it is concluded that the recommendations made were technocratic, in that they assume third parties can 'manufacture agency' to bring about improvements in the behaviour of other people.
- This is a flawed assumption, only, what support there was from the political left lay in support for its recommendations, regardless of the fury reserved for its substantive conclusions.
- Two rival takes from the Runnymede Trust and the Labour Party are examined and found wanting.
- Kemi Badenoch's claim that the United Kingdom is 'one of the best countries in the world to be a black person' is scrutinised empirically.
- Drawing on data from other countries, it is found that ethnic minority individuals fare better here than in the familial countries of origin, in terms of life expectancy, education, wealth, opportunity and happiness. Black people in this country fare much better than in other European countries.
- The report then turns to the fortunes of the 'white working-class', arguing that they are not a 'victim group'. It is shown that government interventions, such as 'graduatisation' and the apprenticeships levy, have penalised working-class people by increasing the costs of getting on in life, as well as causing the supply of apprenticeships to dry up.
- Analysis of the fallout from the recent European football championships shows the level of racial abuse aimed at black English players was low, and much of it from overseas. It is argued that the 'taking of the knee' is a symbolic gesture that antagonises football fans.

Introduction

'In a world where truth means so little, and headstrong preconceptions seem to be all that matter, what hope is there for rational words or rational behaviour, much less mutual understanding across racial lines?' – Thomas Sowell

'Good things are easily destroyed, but not easily created.' – Roger Scruton

It is without doubt that the Black Lives Matter protests, in response to the death of George Floyd in America in 2020, changed something in British life. This change has been noticeable politically and in terms of how elites have behaved, as well as ordinary people. Perhaps the most telling change has been that professing one's commitment to the value of other people's lives became something to be seen to do. This became symbolised through the newly concocted ritual of 'taking the knee', most notably performed by England's football players and the opposition leader, Sir Keir Starmer.

It has become both fashionable to proclaim that the United Kingdom is a bad place to be black or to have any skin colour other than white. The white ethnic majority has been asked to self-examine and denounce itself as beneficiaries of unearned *privilege,* in essence to become a suspicious ethnic group.

The institutions of the country that guarantee what liberty we have and enjoy further became objects of denunciation, damned as either sites of 'institutional', 'structural' or 'systemic' racism as the mood saw fit. Largely, the evidence for this consisted of either disparate statistical outcomes between groups, or disproportionate outcomes of any given group, relative to their share of the country's population. Matters were compounded by Britain's history of empire and trade in slaves, which were taken to be signs of the country's illegitimate standing today. Statues of men who had once been revered were torn down, damaged, vandalised, or quietly removed by quiescent local officials.

A recent play performed at the National Theatre, *Paradise,* portrayed an unnamed dystopian country, described as a 'land of hope and glory' where 'rampant oppression based on skin colour' is practiced. *The Spectator*'s critic described it as 'full of bitterness and misanthropy', and yet at its end, 'the rapturous crowd stood up and roared like mating hyenas.'[1]

This gives some indication of where the opinion of the cultural elite lies, and no doubt this view is popular within such institutions as the BBC and the Civil Service, as well as in the large corporations that dominate the private sector. Yet, polling and survey evidence referenced in this report show that majorities of all races believe this is a good place to live, are happy, and report that despite some tensions, most people tend to get along well. Moreover, the evidence shows both a healthy growth in the size of the minority middle-class, and not just limited to the high performing Chinese and Indian groups. At the same time, substantial numbers believe the Black Lives Matter movement to have worsened race relations.

This is a problem, in that we have an elite which are content, delighted even, to spread falsehoods about how bad things are. To be seen to do so, publicly, is a badge of virtue. This is grave in that their chosen narrative rests on white people as a privileged ethnic group, as evidenced by disparate outcomes and that the time-honoured institutions that underwrite our freely chosen actions are indefensible and require some unspecified, radical reform.

In the short-term, the unintended consequences for this will be to divert scarce resources away from where they are needed during the crisis brought on by the Covid-19 pandemic, and to destroy the trust that is needed to participate in British life. That this discourse might combine with radical Islamist ones, strengthening their argument that this is a country hostile to Muslims, potentially leading to more young people to commit unspeakable acts of violence, is seldom considered.

Longer-term consequences are harder to predict, but it is possible to imagine the current fashionable doctrines of critical race theory fuelling further conflicts.

Consider the following extract from *White Privilege* by Kalwant Bhopal as emblematic of this strain of elite thought:

> 'The prevalence and predominance of whiteness and white privilege work to perpetuate the inferior and powerless position of black and minority ethnic groups – **to keep them in their place**. Whiteness works to maintain and protect white privilege – at all costs – consequently systems and structures are designed to do this.'[2]

What is whiteness if not white people? Bhopal has no answer, and were this to specify Jewishness and Jewish privilege instead, would we tolerate it?

Bhopal describes higher education in particular as rigged to the benefit of whites, as a site of institutional racism that seeks to maintain racial and class domination. Yet she acknowledges in her book the support and kindness she has received from colleagues, including white ones. Her book works primarily on the tautology of the presumption that disparate outcomes between individuals aggregated into groups is both evidence of a *thing* called white privilege and caused by it.

We have seen companies declare their support for Black Lives Matter, regardless of the fact there is a radical political movement that goes by this name, that favours the abolition of the family, of capitalism and the 'defunding' of the police.[3] Advertisers have fallen over themselves to include black people, who at the last census made up around three per cent of the population. This is companies using people, their blackness, to project a corporate image of caring and responsibility. Their promotion of radical identity politics is anything but.

Against this backdrop, we had what came to be known as the Sewell report. This was the culmination of the work of the Commission on Racial and Ethnic Disparities (CRED), a government-appointed commission announced by Boris Johnson and set up under the direction of No. 10 Policy Unit head, Munira Mirza. The Commission was made up of accomplished individuals from various professions and chaired by Tony Sewell, who is an educationalist and founder of the charity *Generating Genius*, and in whose name the report has come to be known.

The report was presented as a continuation of previous government work begun under David Cameron and continued by Theresa May. There is some truth to this, but it is truer to say that the Sewell report was a substantial break from the direction previously travelled in. Past government reviews, most notably May's *Race Disparity Audit*, had outlined what statistical differences there were between groups but had not resulted in much by way of either explanation for why they persisted, or policy. However, what changed was the personnel involved: out went May and her chief adviser on race, long-time anti-racism activist Simon Woolley, and in came Johnson and Mirza.

Mirza had been critical of May's approach, as well as having in the past spoke of institutional racism as both 'a historic legacy here from previous decades', but among 'lobbyists and activists', it is a 'perception more than a reality' that proves corrosive.[4] It is those latter words that so often get presented, shorn of those that qualify them. This is done to present her as politically unacceptable, in that she denies the existence of institutional racism. It is fair to say, however, that she and her allies wanted a break from May and Cameron's approach.

Similar misrepresentation is reserved for Tony Sewell, who is often reported, for example by Sky News, to have said 'evidence of the existence of institutional racism was "flimsy"'.[5] In fact, his exact words in an article for *Prospect* were, 'much of the supposed evidence of institutional racism is flimsy' – words used before criticising the popular interpretation of one specific study.[6]

Such misrepresentations were dredged up to discredit the Commission before its work had even begun. Labour's David Lammy MP described the Commission as 'written on the back of a fag packet'. Pre-emptive critics saw fit to dictate what the report should say, with the Institute of Race Relations stipulating, 'Any enquiry into inequality has to acknowledge structural and systemic factors'.[7]

When the report finally arrived in April 2021, it triggered a mass of outrage and criticism. There was a notional queue of activists, academics, celebrities and politicians outside *The Guardian,* waiting to let fly. The report was widely presented on the cultural and political left as having been thoroughly discredited in a manner without precedent. It was further said to have found no evidence of institutional racism, although that is in fact a moot point, with that statement more attributable to comments Sewell made in a BBC interview or No. 10 briefings, which have proven hard to track down.

In truth, the most prominent critiques were wide of the mark, and often not really bound by any standards of rational or empirical inquiry, as I show in the next chapter. All too often, the critique was that the report ignored 'the lived experience', as though either anecdotal evidence or personal perceptions of unfairness were necessary and sufficient to explain objective facts. That is in contravention of all scientific standards.

It was almost as if something *sacred* had been violated and in order to rectify this they had to say something, anything, to restore the cosmic order. What that violation was exactly, was the perception that suffering had been denied, and that in doing so the government was further oppressing ethnic minority people, that it was 'gaslighting' them.

On top of this, however, was a thinly veiled financial interest. Anti-racism is big business, with many campaigners and politicians deriving their income from trying to stop it.

As the open racism of individuals has declined since the 1980s, so anti-racism campaigners have had to find new forms to fight. 'Structural' and 'institutional' racism, that are supposedly evidenced by disparate outcomes between groups, prove ample grounds for interventions, such as 'unconscious bias training' and 'mandatory ethnicity pay gap reporting', that always promise equality of outcomes, only never quite manage to deliver.

Then along came Sewell, who said, in effect, whatever problems there were, they were largely not to do with race but rather other factors, and specifically, not the racism of white people, institutions, or structures. Crucially, he identified family breakdown, most pronounced among black people, as the cause of disparate outcomes. If this were to become the government's official line on race, then there would be no need for the state to pay for anti-racism workers. You see the problem and why, for so many, the Sewell report had to go.

But once the furore has passed, the critics will have to deal with unintended consequences. By demonising the report to such a hysterical degree, they have only created a level of infamy that guarantees the Sewell report to be the one to endure, to be read by subsequent generations, if only to see how 'awful' it is, and not the orthodox McGregor-Smith review or the generally inconclusive Lammy review.

Whatever its positives and negatives, the critics have made the Sewell report. When people read it, they will find it reasonable and thorough, disputable but certainly an advance on what the American academic Thomas Sowell calls the 'invincible fallacy', namely that differences between ethnic groups are necessarily down to the oppression of one by the other, which sustains the anti-racism racket. Hopefully, they will come to realise they have been lied to, and that whatever anger they might have felt at Sewell might better be directed at those who promise the world, to overcome the very real discrimination that exists in British life, and offer, at considerable expense, things like 'unconscious bias training' and unsurprisingly, achieve nothing.

Demonstrative of the political conflict going on today within our institutions is the recent publication of a document by the Department of Business, Energy, and Industrial Strategy (BEIS), called *Net Zero transition: gender, race and social inclusion – literature review*. It reportedly said 'the BLM movement has drawn attention to the structural inequalities and institutional racism that low carbon transitions must navigate.' Widely ridiculed, the report was withdrawn the next day, with an anonymous government source telling *Guido Fawkes*, 'Compiling dross like this has become an industry in itself in the Civil Service and it's got to stop.'[8] The BEIS report gives us some indication of what is the default and dogmatic mode within the state and how at odds Sewell stood with it.

This report is written as a follow up to an earlier work I had written for Civitas called *How we think about disparity and what we get wrong* (2020).[9] I had read every government-backed review authored under Conservative-led governments to date. I pointed out the key concerns and assumptions that lay behind whatever conclusions and recommendations made, and found them wanting.

I had not wished to return to the subject since it is pretty much a joyless one. You start off with the assumption that ethnic minorities are being cheated, but the more you look into the evidence, you find it insufficient to sustain that conclusion as the sole explanation. This is because much of the evidence is 'flimsy', like Sewell says, in that it is usually based on claims that ethnic minority people have worse outcomes, only there are some groups who experience all the bad things but do better regardless, such as Jews, Chinese, Indians, and certain sections of black Africans. If this is systemic racism, then we are not very good at it.

Disparate outcomes may be down to discrimination, they may not be, but you cannot really tell just by looking at statistics on outcomes, or via methods of analysis that rest on correlations and in effect look to identify causes of outcomes from other outcomes. But what about their antecedents? Positive disparate outcomes that favour certain ethnic minority groups do not preclude the existence of the grand racisms of the institutions or the structures, whatever these may be, nor do they evidence them. More importantly, they are not really consistent with the idea of a racially closed society.

The literature on the matter is seldom rewarding and often poor in quality; take Bhopal's *White Privilege,* which you will find widely promoted, including, until recently, by the governmental equality regulator, the Equality and Human Rights Commission, as a 'good book' both morally and qualitatively. It is neither.

Things are seldom proven, conclusions are predetermined as a matter of faith over fact, all fuelled by an unjustified belief that its proponents are doing good and not just lining their pockets. Concepts that are morally loaded and should be concisely and logically defined, the building blocks of social science, are seldomly so. All too often you find yourself dealing with a lexicon of neologisms or bastardisations of the English language that leave you chasing shadows. You try to pin an opponent down, only the terms are not defined and will shift from one writer to another and may mean something new tomorrow.

Tony Sewell observed that 'institutional' racism has become a 'catch-all phrase' used to describe everything and anything to do with racism. But that is nothing new, with scholars having noticed this since at least the 1980s. The problems of language are confounded in that the penalties for one false move are severe. Take, for example, the case of Noah Carl, whose academic career has been ruined after he was sacked by the University of Cambridge, following students' objections to an article he had written arguing why it may not be such a good idea to suppress evidence on differences in intelligence between racial groups.[10]

Whatever you might think of such research, and there are real moral dilemmas to it, disparity on intelligence tests is an age-old finding of psychology and the moral conundrum does not go away just because Carl does. What we have is the new rule that the measure of scientific legitimacy is whether or not the findings offend us, as though we had a right for the empirical world to conform to our beliefs as to what is proper. Ultimately, this is a discourse in which there is severely limited freedom but no consideration that through repression of ugly facts, we hide from ourselves what may be the better and more moral course of action. This new rule has been imposed by cowardly academics afraid of the ignorant students they are paid to enlighten.

I felt compelled to return to the topic, however, in light of the Sewell report and the furore it provoked since they both interested me. There were also certain ideas that occurred to me, or events which I thought of importance that I wished to pass comment upon. This report is thus a short collection of essays, from which a common thread is extracted.

Both Sewell and his critics are examined (Chapter 1). In addition to pointing out the inadequacy of the critics, I make the case they doubly blundered in *agreeing* with Sewell's recommendations, which are largely technocratic, necessitating further government interventions in matters where it has limited competence.

Put simply, government cannot make you love your wife and stick by her, especially when so many figures within our present government seem to fall out of love with their own, or love somebody else's. It simply does not have enough knowledge about individuals, nor control of them, to engineer an equality of outcomes. This is Sewell's aim, despite acknowledging the cause is not to do with race. His break with orthodoxy is only partial in that regard.

I then examine what the left wishes Sewell had said, in the form of two reports, one from Labour (Lawrence Review) and one from the Runnymede Trust (Chapter 2). These are based on the insistence of the fact of structural and institutional racism, and nothing more. The exercise is undertaken in the public interest, in that we need to know what the left's own proposals are and in what ways they are insufficient.

Rather than looking to explain disparity and to come up with some perfect plan to close it, I attempt to gauge the openness of British life in terms of race. My point of departure is a comment made by government minister Kemi Badenoch, that the United Kingdom is 'one of the best countries in the world to be a black person'. I wanted to know if this was true and how it might be empirically validated. Comparisons are made between the typical black person in this country and with his comparator in other, majority black, countries, along with similar comparisons for other ethnic groups. I also examine survey evidence of the lives of black people living in European countries.

The picture presented is that they, along with other minority groups, do substantially better here than elsewhere, evidenced by greater life expectancy, wealth, happiness, better education, and opportunity. I further note the growth of the minority middle-class to show the extent to which despite the 'drag' of ethnic discrimination or racially motivated abuse and violence, it is nowhere near sufficient to arrest the momentum.

There are real costs to being an ethnic minority in Britain, either in terms of racial verbal or physical abuse, or the costs associated with homophily, or those subtle and empirically illusive feelings of not belonging.

But the evidence shows the most egregious offences to be both rare and declining, although not sufficiently so as to preclude the fact that most minority people will experience something unpleasant in their life time. The evidence also shows this is largely a matter of numbers, with 'minority' individuals more likely to meet a 'majority' bigot than *vice versa*. For people from ethnic minorities can harbour prejudice and racial animosity too, sometimes more so than the white ethnic majority, as demonstrated by Muslim anti-Semitism and the disproportionate black involvement in 'hate crime' prosecutions and convictions.

Nor is there any reason why we should expect zero racism when it is so loosely defined, since there is no reason why two groups should take to each other, especially when the majority group has not consented to the mass immigration that sustains and grows the minority population, and which has a legitimate expectation of integration that is often widely ignored. Cordial relations based on an asymmetry of expectations imposed from on high, that white people, no matter what, are a suspicious group, while 'grooming gangs' and Islamist segregation are politely ignored, will not happen. If relations between the oldest established ethnic groups in the country are *still* strained, between the English and Scottish most notably, why should we expect perfect relations with relative newcomers?

Ultimately it is concluded that the benefits outweigh the costs; that is why people jump in unseaworthy crafts to come to Europe from Africa and Asia, but do not feel content to stop in France, preferring one more perilous journey (Chapter 3). It follows that government interventions that look to force minority advance even further are not really needed – people manage on their own, well enough. Forcing the matter necessitates waste and risks breaking the 'system' that works for so many.

Evidence is presented to show that relatively poor people

of Pakistani origin in Britain have more wealth than the typical Pakistani in Pakistan. The same is true for nearly all ethnic minority groups within this country, relative to individuals in their familial countries of origin. Proponents of 'structural racism' present disparity between minority groups and the white British ethnic majority as evidence for this, and point to our institutions as somehow causal. But the disparity between the British Pakistani and the Pakistani Pakistani needs to be explained too, and this likely rests on the institutions that govern our life. Those radicals who demand an always unspecified revolutionary reform must bear in mind that we do have something that has allowed ethnic minority individuals to flourish. As Sir Roger Scruton said, good things are more easily destroyed than they are created.

I then turn to discourses on the 'white-working-class', in response to a recent parliamentary report on their supposed abandonment that said they are let down and 'left behind'. This, I argue, is worryingly beginning to look like politicians of the right playing identity politics *standing on its head,* in that they have identified their own victim group for which they can advocate for in hope of securing block votes.

I further show that politicians have penalised the working-class through increasing the costs of getting on, which makes it now necessary to acquire a university education to join the professions, where often before, it was not. Their meddling has further caused the supply of apprenticeships to dry up through the imposition of a levy on employers that was supposed to increase it (Chapter 4).

The potential for our misunderstanding of things, of our willingness to see only the worst, came to a head at the recent European Championships in football (2021). Two issues were of importance, firstly the impulse to believe the racist abuse of the three black English players who missed penalties was as much as a torrent when it was more a trickle, largely coming from overseas. Secondly, 'the taking of the knee'; the ritual of going down on one knee which provoked sections of the fans booing and in conflict with the very same players they were supposed to be supporting.

Racism has become *The Great Evil*, so much so that we lose our sense of perspective. At the same time, the liberal elites take such rituals as sacrosanct and their non-observance as *desecration*, without bothering to ask why Millwall fans can boo kneeling one week but the next, cheer an anti-racism banner. The problem is the gesture for liberals is seen as symbolic of the moral value of preventing harm and suffering, but for socially-conservatively-minded fans, who have patriotic pride and not the elite's national revulsion that Orwell spoke of, it is seen as symbolic of shame and self-repudiation of which the majority of die-hard fans want no part.

Identity politics is capturing our national game and seeking to impose a new 'moral code' on football fans, whereby the game is transformed into a vehicle for promoting 'social justice'. What they are accomplishing is turning it into a round of finger pointing, at odds with the values of supporters, which is tragic in that they sour what ought to be moments of national unity. This shows the potential for identity politics to ruin a nation (Chapter 5).

Finally, and by way of a conclusion, I take a look at some of those salacious dead white men who dominate unduly the sociological canon they did so much to found. My purpose is to try and correct the way we think about disparity. Sewell sees the explanation for one variable to be found in another; for example, poor educational performance is to be explained by family breakdown and fatherlessness, resulting in disparate ethnic outcomes for those groups most effected. But there is no 'mechanism' or explanation as to how; to join the dots.

I saw a parallel here to the work of Emile Durkheim, who sought to explain one 'social fact' by another, in opposition to Max Weber who sought explanation for purposeful human behaviour in the individual psyche. Doing so not only provides a genuine explanation, but also the basis for which we might construct arguments for better behaviour that are likely persuasive. Government cannot repair the family through the endeavours of academics and civil servants when the individuals concerned are not convinced of its value.

I further identify Durkheim's concept of *anomie*, meaning the absence of rules, as having the potential to theoretically explain much of the malaise among the British population, that is more pronounced among black and poor white groups than Asians. Moreover, I point to the Marxian influence on radical identity politics, in which group disparity between classes is explained by an exploitative system, as too are disparate outcomes on any other given variable: ethnicity, sex, sexuality and so on. This is something common with the most extreme political ideologies, including those of the far-right, meaning these are all part of the same family of ideas, that differ only in the severity of the remedies proposed and the extent to which they are acceptable in polite society. Marx's influence is further felt in that, like him, today's radicals are full of complaints but offer no clue as to what their perfect world would look like (Chapter 6).

My conclusion is that we have something good but imperfect in this country. Ethnic minority people do well, better than anywhere else, and have flourished here. This is why more and more wish to come here and not remain in

France. The facts show racism is real but small in magnitude and exists despite the institutions, not because of them.

Our institutions are precious, delicate and easily ruined. Yet a belief has developed that the best thing we can do is complain; that the most noble thing one can do is to complain without any specification of what is to come next or weighing up of both the positives and negatives. When pressed, the only response is to empower political activists, a cultural vanguard, within institutions or enact ideological programmes in places such as the NHS and BBC. But this is a problem in that such individuals are neither accountable to the electorate nor bound by a commitment to neutrality. Moreover, unelected bureaucrats start to impose political expectations that are contested, on free individuals within the institutions, either as employees or as service users. Elites start to impose change with penalties for non-compliance. After all, who wants to be the one not to wear the rainbow lanyard?

This is a selfish and irresponsible thing to do that will only lead well-meaning people away from where their efforts might bear fruit and their careers prove fulfilling. It has potential to foster the withdrawal of consent from democratic governance, pitting ethnic groups against each other. Anti-racism, in its traditional sense, exists on the premise that racism can fuel the most-obscene forms of persecution and bloodshed. The historical record backs that up. We believe we must punish severely even relatively innocuous utterances, yet it has become fashionable to bandy about such notions as 'white privilege' and 'white guilt' as though they are not harmful ideas. Certainly, we know from history that notions of collective guilt and unearned 'privilege' have fuelled persecution of Jews.

Radical reform risks ruining everything, piecemeal reform

will only engender useless interventions like unconscious bias training, that only blunt our economic dynamism, which is the source of our national wealth.

Ultimately, 'systemic racism' is unprovable since it cannot be evidenced or falsified if the argument is to be won or lost on what disparate outcomes between groups really mean. But if you remain unconvinced, rest assured, you may not like our supposed 'systemic racism' but the remedy may prove much worse. In truth, it is a strange situation to be in where we are all so pessimistic when the evidence gives so much cause to be optimistic.

My gratitude is expressed to Civitas and to all those who contributed to the production of this report. In this report, I often use 'Sewell' as shorthand for the Sewell report. While he is the lead author of it and ultimately responsible, I do not mean to suggest the work represents his own personal views in their entirety.

1.

'Hell hath no fury' – the Sewell Report and its aftermath

Introduction

What came to be known as the Sewell report was commissioned by Boris Johnson in the summer of 2020, in response to the Black Lives Matter protests, at the same time we were under lockdown due to the Covid-19 pandemic. The proper title of the report is: *Commission on Race and Ethnic Disparities: The Report*. It looked at differences of outcome between ethnic groups, what we call 'disparities', and sought to find explanations for them.

This chapter looks at the report's content before examining the heated criticism that it received, finding it mostly to be completely unwarranted, often woefully so. No judgement is made on the conclusions of the report, in terms of explaining *why disparity of outcomes exists*, other than to say it is reasonable to expect, given groups are different in so many ways.

All the critics missed the point, that the recommendations are based on the assumption that disparate outcomes are a problem to be solved and can be done so through technocratic interventions. This is a doubtful tenet. Indeed, if any political consensus was to be found, it was in support of what are a set of recommendations made by Sewell and his colleagues, based on the *belief* they will bring about improvements in other people's behaviour, not evidence.

What did Sewell actually say?

The report acknowledged that while disparity existed between ethnic groups, this seldom had its roots in racism. Instead, it could be attributed to other factors such as family structure, geography or levels of aspiration, termed 'immigrant optimism'. It looked at four broad areas: employment, education, health and crime/policing.

Noting that black Caribbean children had relatively poor performance in school, while black African children did reasonably well, it said:

> 'As their Caribbean peers sit in the same classrooms, it is difficult to blame racism in education for [their] underachievement.'

Racism both exists in the country and is a 'real force in the UK', but is of less importance than other factors in shaping your life chances, according to the Sewell report. The report further noted that many of the least successful, the poorest, were white.

In his foreword, Sewell refers to Linton Kwesi Johnson, who spoke of black Britain as having two phases, namely the 'heroic' and the 'rebel'. The former pertained to those newcomers struggling to find a way in a society that had offered them a home, but did not offer them community.

The rebel generation were largely their children and 'featured running battles with police and a breakdown in community relations'. The report says that the Black Lives Matter protests persisted in this vein, but perhaps gently and implicitly chides the protestors for protesting without the same level of cause.

Sewell speaks of a new phase, namely the 'era of participation', and notes both that ethnic minorities on the whole are better represented in the highest occupational class, while the 'ethnic pay gap' is 2.3 per cent as of 2019.

The report says:

> 'We therefore cannot accept the accusatory tone of much of the current rhetoric on race, and the pessimism about what has been and what more can be achieved.'

On 'institutional racism', the report expresses concern that its definition is 'evolving' from the 1981 Scarman Report on the Brixton riots to the 1999 Macpherson Report into the investigation of the murder of Stephen Lawrence in 1993. Macpherson's definition is said to have 'stood the test of time' and 'described a set of practices and behaviours that were commonplace, sanctioned by authorities, and which unduly harmed ethnic minority groups – even if unintentionally.' It notes that police are actively trawling for reports of hate crime as evidence that the police are no longer institutionally racist, since they are obviously, now, taking it seriously.

'Institutional racism' is now 'being liberally used, and often to describe any circumstances in which differences in outcomes between racial and ethnic groups exist in an institution, without evidence…'. This only serves to devalue the charge, while leading us to ignore other problems, according to Sewell.

'Institutional racism' is used interchangeably with 'structural' and 'systemic' racism, according to Sewell, which creates 'further confusion', reducing the chances of successful remedy. Its use may relate to 'specific processes which can be identified', but may also 'relate to the feeling described by many ethnic minorities of "not belonging"'.

The report acknowledges 'a class of actions, behaviours and incidents at organisational level which cause ethnic minorities to want for a sense of belonging', known as being 'othered', but that this has a highly subjective dimension, making it difficult to substantiate. It instead looks to provide definitions that would allow for objective quantification.

If further states:

> 'Terms like "Structural Racism" have roots in a critique of capitalism, which states that racism is inextricably linked to capitalism. So, by that definition, until that system is abolished racism will flourish. Many are using "Structural Racism" to mean deep-seated exclusion rather than the tearing down of capitalism.'

This is significant in that it shows how a term may be unescapably radical and revolutionary in origin, but used by people who are neither, to mean something else. Thus, when you try and address it on the terms of its inception, it is taken as offensively dismissive of everyday problems of real people. Perhaps this lies at the root of so much of the *popular* anger at Sewell, in that people were talking at cross-purposes.

Sewell then provides succinct definitions which are recommended for official use:

> 'Institutional racism: applicable to an institution that is racist or discriminatory process, policies, attitudes or behaviours in a single institution.
>
> 'Systemic racism: this applies to interconnected organisations, or wider society, which exhibit racist or discriminatory processes, policies, attitudes or behaviours.
>
> 'Structural racism: to describe a legacy of historic racist or discriminatory processes, policies, attitudes or behaviours that continue to shape organisations and societies today.'

While these are succinct and better than the verbosity of Macpherson that serves to obscure the concept being discussed, I would take issue with the definition proposed for structural racism, in that it is hard to think of what could not be described as such a 'legacy', making it unescapable no matter what remedies are sought.

While the report offers a couple of empirical indicators for institutional racism, it has little more to say, other than that to keep banging on about this without precise definition will only sow further animosity and distrust. In its empirical chapters, the concept is scarcely mentioned, nor is it told how one can discount it as an explanation for disparate outcomes.

However, implicitly, this is done; for example, in the case of education by looking at outcomes and observing that not all ethnic minority groups do badly, indeed most surpass the white majority in terms of the progress they make. The empirical data are simply not consistent with the image of a society that seeks to denigrate and frustrate those who are not white. The report then makes recommendations for government, which should form the basis for future policy (these are discussed in some detail below) but first, some of the more prominent criticisms of Sewell are addressed.

The critics

This section examines some of the more prominent as well as empirically driven critiques. There were some who rejected the report because it seemed to go against the value of recognising suffering as a first step towards alleviating it. For others it appeared to fly in the face of truth. At times it appeared as though deliberately inflammatory comments were made. Perhaps the most egregious take on the report was that it somehow glorified slavery. This view was put about by Labour MP Marsha de Cordova, who was at the time the party's spokeswoman for women and equalities.

She said:

> 'The government must urgently explain how they came to publish content which glorifies the slave trade and immediately dissociate themselves with these remarks'.[11]

All that was said in the report was:

> 'There is a new story about the Caribbean experience which speaks to the slave period not only being about profit and suffering, but how culturally African people transferred themselves into a re-modelled African/Britain'.

That is the only reference to slavery in the report. It was written in the context of expressing the idea that children from ethnic minority groups come from cultures that are hybrid and have British roots, and that this could be the common ground for a school curriculum that sought conciliation and not divisiveness and repudiation. It was about trying to tell a unifying story.

E.P. Thompson in his seminal work, *The making of the English working-class*, sought to portray a heroic working-class – people who were present at their own inception, who shaped their own culture despite extremely trying circumstances. All Sewell was doing was speaking in a similar way about West Indians. A subsequent article published in *The Guardian* newspaper, by the respected historian David Olusoga, revealed there is nothing controversial about the argument the Commission made, and that there is in fact consensus behind it:

> '... the authors state that the "slave period" of Caribbean history" was not only "about profit and suffering". Well, of course it wasn't. Every historian of slavery I have ever encountered writes about Britain's slave-trading and slave-

owning as a history of resistance and resilience in which people trafficked from their homelands or born into bondage created new cultures, identities and art forms, while being dehumanised and commodified'.[12]

Olusoga is more incensed by the report's grammar, supposed historical illiteracy, as well as alleging the use of an argument used by slave owners to justify slavery, that 'by becoming culturally British, black people were somehow beneficiaries of the system'.

The report makes no such argument. Nor is the report about history, and not one to which a historian's skill set is most attuned to critiquing. Mostly, Olusoga's critique of the report rests on parsing what will inevitably feature moments of poor prose, since it is written by a committee. Olusoga does not engage with the report where it is strongest; he neglects to scrutinise its evidential base and fails to ask if the recommendations made will work.

The Sewell report was also denounced by the 'United Nations Working Group of Experts on People of African Descent'. Such a body is not the voice of the United Nations, but rather a group of individuals whose work is funded by it. The critique was then bandied about as though the United Nations *proper* had issued a stern rebuke, when no such thing had occurred.

The group writes:

'Among other things, the Report blames single parents for poor outcomes, ignoring the racial disparities and the racialized nature of poor outcomes that exist despite an increased prevalence of single-parent families in every demographic.'[13]

This is what the Sewell report says:

'... this is **not** about allocating blame, but simply pointing out that children require both time and resources, and that is more likely to be available when both parents play active roles in their upbringing.'

It should be pointed out that some ethnic groups have relatively strong outcomes as well as low levels of single parenthood. As the report shows, just six per cent of British Indian children grow up in single parent families, compared to 63 per cent of black Caribbean children. Academic evidence is cited in the report linking father absence to 'worse educational performance, emotional development, and adult mental health', as well as criminality. At the same time, it allows for the fact that many children are raised successfully in single parent families.

The United Nations' experts blunder further on:

> 'Similarly, the Report's call for "a more responsible use of statistics," and its conclusion that hate crime incidents are decreasing even as hate crime reports increase, is speculative and convenient rather than being a necessary, accurate, or responsible interpretation of the data sets.'

The United Nations' experts have missed the point in this regard, nor have they grasped what the report actually says:

> 'Although it is often believed that hate crime is rising sharply, the most reliable data shows that it may be declining. There were 76,070 race-related hate crimes recorded by police in England and Wales in 2019, up 131 per cent since 2011 to 2012.
>
> 'But according to the more robust Crime Survey of England and Wales (CSEW), racially motivated hate crimes went down from 149,000 in 2010/12 to 104,000 in 2018/20. While the decline is significant the figures still show that a sizeable number of incidents take place.'

In no way is the report 'relying' on police data, quite the opposite, and it is proper to privilege the Crime Survey over police reports when inferring historical trends. This is standard practice in criminology; it is what any undergraduate criminologist learns, and no serious criminologist would entertain otherwise. This is because police data are subject to the willingness to report as well as political prompting. Moreover, the Commission was simply repeating the verdict of the Office for National Statistics (ONS).[14]

The United Nations' critique is almost impossible to respond to fully, in that it is littered with academic jargon that makes an argument difficult to detect and respond to, or is based on indignation and assertion without evidence.[15]

Another eminent critic was Sir Michael Marmot, who is a professor of epidemiology at University College London, voicing his disquiet in *The Guardian*. His complaint is that the report selectively cited his research in that it references his *Marmot Review* (2010) but not his *Health Equity in England: The Marmot Review 10 Years On* (2020) or *Build Back Fairer: The Covid-19 Marmot Review* (2020). It should be considered that Sewell only referenced the Marmot Review to point out its lack of conclusion on ethnic disparity, situating itself within the existing policy literature, and no more. It is unfair to claim this amounted to that it 'quoted my views'.[16]

He claimed that were his more recent work included, then this would have led to a different conclusion. However, it should be pointed out that *10 Years On* mentions 'racism' just once. As he makes clear in his *Guardian* article, he became a convert to the idea of structural racism through a study of the Americas. As Marmot writes, 'This thinking on structural racism informed our interpretation of evidence on health in the UK', but that hardly seems sufficient.

Perusing, *Build Back Fairer* reveals structural racism is undefined, other than to say it is 'the causes of the causes of the causes'. Largely its presence is confirmed by the assertion of its authors. But then, how do you prove structural racism caused something which caused something else, which caused something else? When Marmot ever gets close to evidencing his claims, you get something like this:

> 'Long-standing evidence shows that structural racism is at the heart of worse living and working conditions for BAME communities, which leads to worse health – in turn this will lead to a higher risk of Covid-19 mortality.
>
> 'BAME groups face discrimination in different spheres of their lives, such as employment, working conditions and earnings, which leads to lower incomes, higher levels of stress and higher poverty rates than those experienced by White British populations, and high rates of some health conditions'.[17]

The paper cited by Marmot to justify the claim of 'long-standing evidence' is by James Nazroo et al. and is largely a conceptual review that fails to define what structural racism is, despite this being fundamental to its purpose. Ample evidence is presented for differences between groups, but nothing to explain why this is 'structural racism'. Where there should be a clear explication, instead the terms get vague:

> 'Importantly, structural racism consists of not just material, but also cultural and ideological dimensions... The circulation of ideas and representations that produce race and ethnic groups as different, but also as threatening and inferior, serve to rationalise and inform an uneven distribution of resources. They comprise the co-constitution of material with symbolic denigration.'[18]

The supposition of Marmot's *Build Back Fairer*, that structural racism causes differentials in the standard of living which then causes differences between groups, cannot account for why it is only *some* health conditions and not *all*. The

Public Health England Covid-19 statistical review showed in normal times white Britons had worse mortality.[19] The Sewell report showed ample evidence of ethnic minority groups having better mortality from some diseases, worse for others. Why does structural racism produce worse outcomes, but only selectively?

Marmot's work is based on the premise that all social groups should have equal outcomes despite their being different on so many indicators, and if they do not, it is unjust and they can be made to have them, through the direction of people like him. But the folly of his work is proven in *10 Years On*, in which he praised Norway for its 'proportionate universalist' policies to reduce what he calls 'inequalities' in health, and yet:

> 'The persistence of health inequalities [in Norway] despite these integrated approaches has led some to suggest a more proportionate universalist approach might more effectively address the needs of those with fewer years of education.'

His *Guardian* article reveals much about his elitist thinking:

> 'The [Sewell] report's authors recognise the importance of social determinants of health but want to look downstream at what individuals and communities can do for themselves. What? If you find yourself in unaffordable housing or in-work poverty, do what you can to get out of it?'[20]

But those who are successful in life or have even a basic level of comfort have done certain things in order to get there. If they did not do such things, then they would be in poverty. The lifestyles they enjoy are not the gift of university professors but stem from a commitment to work, education and positive social and family relationships. Why can this not be an expectation for others too?

Another notable denunciation of the Sewell report came

from Mohammad S. Razai, Azeem Majeed and Aneez Esmail, all academics specialising in healthcare. Their complaint was published in *The British Medical Journal* and was promoted in *The Guardian* under the headline, 'No 10's race report used 'cherry-picked' data, say public health experts'.[21]

Reading *The BMJ* article reveals it to be confected fury along with the insistence that differences between groups must be down to structural racism, and nothing more. Razai et al. claim that the scientific consensus is that 'ethnic minorities have the worst health outcomes on almost all health parameters'.[22] They charge that the Commission lacked the expertise to deal with this issue and that it should have been peer-reviewed by independent experts, and that the Commission had pre-determined conclusions.

It is true that the Commission lacked a medical scientist. That is why they enlisted the help of Raghib Ali, Avirup Chowdhury, Nita Forouhi and Nick Wareham of the MRC Epidemiology Unit at the University of Cambridge to review the evidence on ethnic disparity in health outcomes. These are independent medical scientists who owe the government or Tony Sewell et al. no favours. Together, they reviewed 125 different sources of scientific evidence, for the most part peer-reviewed articles in scientific journals.[23]

Here are just some examples of what they found:

- Nearly all ethnic minority groups had significantly better premature mortality for both men and women;
- Minority groups can have *both* better and worse mortality depending on the disease in question;
- Evidence from Scotland on outcomes within the NHS shows minority outcomes are often equal, sometimes better, sometimes worse.

On this last point, Razai et al. are at pains to discredit the use of Scottish data since only a minority of minorities live there. But why should NHS Scotland be any different from the rest of the country? The claim of the scientific consensus showing worse health outcomes is also wrong. Moreover, the Cambridge scientists show all minority groups are much less likely to die by suicide. How the proponents of the structural racism explanation might account for this is an interesting question.

Another critique was offered by Alan Manning and Rebecca Rose of the London School of Economics. They present data to show 'over the past 25 years, the overriding impression is of stasis', in contradiction to the Sewell report's claim of 'overall convergence story on employment and pay'.[24] I would probably agree with them on pay; that is what is shown by Longhi and Brynin's data (2017).[25] But to be fair to Sewell, it does say:

> 'The [ethnicity] pay gap [defined as white versus all minority groups] … is at its lowest level since 2012 at 2.3 per cent.'

That is consistent with claims of 'overall convergence'. However, the figures for unemployment rates presented by Manning and Rose defy expectation in that they show no bulge in disparity between white and minority groups during the 'Great Recession' of the late 2000s/early 2010s as is both evidenced in official statistics and in past recessions. While Manning and Rose's data show little sign of a trend towards convergence on the white average, this is not what is shown by Yaojun Li's data, taken in part from the same data source – the Labour Force Survey. His data encompass a wider time frame and clearly show convergence, as seen in the graph below.

Manning and Rose present nine-year rolling averages

which should have the effect of smoothing out the trend. This may have the effect of making any convergence appear less pronounced, since the extremes of any given year are 'mellowed' out. Yet, close inspection of Manning and Rose's graphs shows erratic changes between years, not consistent with the smoothing effects of a rolling average, implying something has gone wrong with their data.

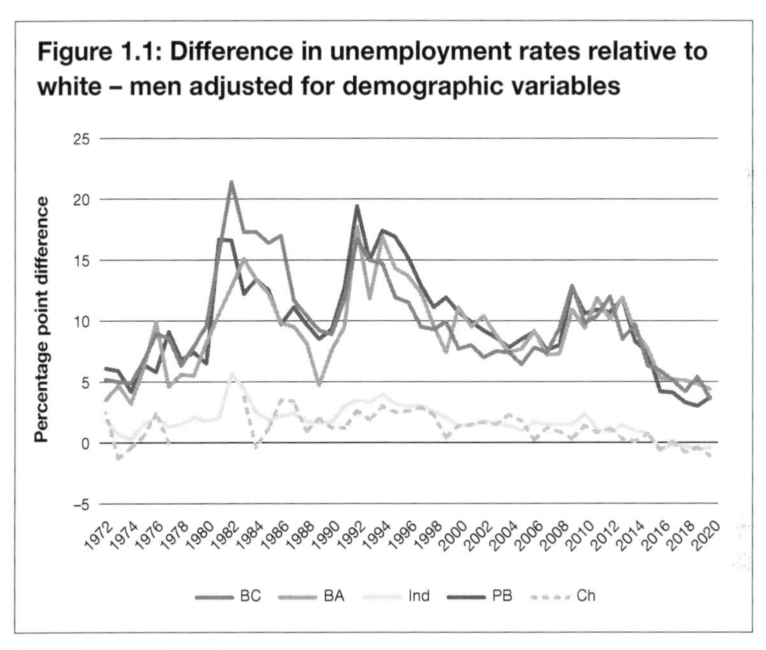

Figure 1.1: Difference in unemployment rates relative to white – men adjusted for demographic variables

Source: GHS/LFS/Yaojun Li.

Moreover, Manning and Rose ignore Li's evidence presented to Sewell's commission, on 'social mobility' which showed:

> 'With the exception of men from the black Caribbean and combined Pakistani and Bangladeshi ethnic groups, most ethnic groups are now broadly level with the white ethnic group in terms of occupational class'.[26]

The old guard

Next up to denounce the report was Simon Woolley, who founded Operation Black Vote and used to oversee the government's policy on race during the 'burning injustices' years of Theresa May. For his efforts, he was knighted and given a peerage, and is now head of Homerton College, Cambridge.

His complaint published in *The Guardian* is that this was a wasted opportunity to propose policies to end racism.[27] It should be pointed out, however, that when he was shaping the government's policy on race, one of the criticisms made of his *Race Disparity Audit* was the distinct lack of policies.[28] The mantra was 'explain or change', only there was no explanation and no change. That Woolley has argued that nothing happened is testimony to his own failure. Moreover, for all his pique, the policies that Woolley demands are likely ineffective, for example, mandatory ethnicity pay gap reporting.

As the Sewell report makes clear, this is not easily done since there are 19 ethnic groups defined by the ONS, while sample sizes will be small, meaning companies in places with very small proportions of non-white groups will produce unreliable data. As I have argued previously for Civitas, since the introduction of mandatory gender pay gap reporting for companies over 250 employees, the gap for companies has trickled *upwards*. At the same time, the overall gender pay gap was falling anyway, prior to the intervention.

The policy is wildly illiberal in that companies are required to prove themselves innocent, reversing the standard of the assumption of innocence before proven guilt. The proof they are required to offer could imply discrimination, or simply that the sexes, or ethnic groups for that matter, engaged in different types of labour within companies, which naturally command different rates of pay. Companies are restricted in pursing genuinely meaningful economic goals due to the opportunity cost of meeting the pointless government diktat.[29]

There is a group of people, including Woolley, that is fixated on mandatory ethnicity pay gap reporting. A letter organised by the charity Business in the Community called upon the government to commit to it. Sandra Kerr claimed 'the [Sewell] report was a missed opportunity to confirm the government commitment to implement the McGregor-Smith Review recommendations on mandatory ethnicity pay gap reporting'. It is not true, however, that that review made such a recommendation. Rather it recommended mandatory publication of employee ethnicity, broken down by pay-grade. Moreover, Kerr claimed dubiously, 'companies have been begging the government for a mandatory duty'.[30]

In the parliamentary debate on the Sewell report, Theresa May quoted the chief economist of the Bank of England as saying, 'published pay gaps are a starting point for corporate and national accountability'. They are nothing of the kind. She further asked if the government will 'commit to mandatory reporting of ethnicity pay gaps'.[31] Her own government committed to introducing the measure in its 2017 manifesto, only to push it into the long grass by opening up a public consultation.

In the days before the publication of the Sewell report, *The Guardian* published a story claiming, '[s]everal sources said the commission is expected to urge the government to commit to making annual ethnicity pay reporting mandatory for larger firms'.[32] As it transpired, that was untrue and the Commission did no such thing. Who were these sources and why were they briefing the press on this? Was this not some half-ditched attempt to create facts on the ground?

Lived experience

One of criticisms of the Sewell report, that was delivered with the expectation that it was both clinching and damning, was that it denied the 'lived experience' of ethnic minorities in Britain. For instance, here is *Observer* columnist Sonia Sodha:

> 'I also think the report in terms of its evidential base, underplays the importance of lived experience.'[33]

Others to criticise the Sewell report included London mayor Sadiq Khan, who wrote:

> 'We need to acknowledge and listen to the lived experience of black, Asian, and minority ethnic people in our country, so we can take meaningful action to break down barriers and make our society more equal for everyone.'[34]

Similarly, Labour MP Dianne Abbott:

> 'This is people's lived experience and it is as if this commission... is taking us back in the argument for racial justice, not taking us forward.'[35]

Note that lack of precision and the inability to convey ideas, however soothing the noises might be to political sensibility. How can a society be 'more equal for everyone'? What is 'racial justice' exactly?[36]

The term 'lived experience' is one of those that sneak into common parlance but when parsed closely, appears to make no sense. As Rod Liddle asked on *Spectator TV*, what experience is not lived? It is a neologism, with no clear definition deployed in common parlance. I have seen it used credibly to describe the perspectives of those who are not academic experts, but have a form of knowledge or perspective that is worthwhile seeking out. In this regard, 'lived experience' is a slightly pompous way of saying 'first-hand experience'. It is of value in that it provides something more tangible than the detached expert's appraisal of statistics. The problem is that it may not be typical as well as rest on subjective perceptions. For example, the Bishop of Dover, Rose Hudson-Wilkin, criticised the Sewell report as 'deeply disturbing' and that the 'lived experience' of minority Britons 'tells a different story to that being shared by this report'. She said:

> 'When I walk into major establishments and no longer see black people in a majority as cleaners and servers... then I will be the first one to shout that we are a model for other "white-majority countries".'[37]

But the majority of cleaners as well as kitchen hands are white Britons, at around 65 to 70 per cent. Moreover, the largest minority group within these occupations is 'white other', at around 10 to 17 per cent.[38] The problem is that Hudson-Wilkin is recalling those black cleaners that her own individual walk of life has led her to encounter, but which, as it transpires, are not typical of these occupations on the whole.

From my own 'lived experience' of working in kitchens, I can tell you that the Poles and Czechs I knew were often overqualified for their jobs and worked ferociously hard. There was good reason for this, in that they could drop down professionally in order to earn more than they would back home. In this light, we should not view black people working in kitchens or in service as necessarily bad. It is actually an opportunity from which more can be built. Nevertheless, as Ben Judah's *This is London* shows, many African kitchen porters are exploited and work under conditions that are exhausting as well as demeaning.

According to *Oxford Reference*, 'lived experience' has three uses:

> '(1) Personal knowledge about the world gained through first hand involvement in everyday events...; (2) In phenomenology, our situated, immediate, activities and encounters in everyday experience, prereflexively [sic] taken for granted reality rather than as something perceived or represented; (3) From Althusser's structuralist Marxist perspective, all human activity, which he emphasises is not a given or pure 'reality', but a 'peculiar relationship to the real' which is 'identical with' ideology.'[39]

There is a problem here in that Marxist ideological constructs are going by the same name as things that genuinely exist, namely first-hand experience or perception. What is being referred to when we speak of 'lived experience'? Is it the one or the other? Moreover, Althusser himself was criminally insane, having his own 'peculiar relationship to the real', which led to the murder of his wife.

But in recent times, we have seen the triumph of a new variant of 'lived experience', namely to say that if the individual perceives something to be bad, this is sufficient to trump any factual claims to the contrary. The best example comes from the infamous episode of *Good Morning Britain* where presenters Piers Morgan, Susanna Reid and Alex Beresford were discussing the allegations that the royal family had worried about the colour of the Duke and Duchess of Sussex's then-unborn son, and that he had been denied being a prince because of this. Beresford is an occasional commentator on the show but mostly presents the weather.

> Morgan: 'The first part of that allegation, we don't know any of the details or who said it or how they said it. The second one is completely untrue. Meghan has got it wrong. Archie

> hasn't been preventing from being a prince because of his skin-colour…'.
>
> Beresford: 'But again, it's their lived experience.'
>
> Morgan: 'No, it's not true.'
>
> Beresford: 'This is where the confusion comes in, in how do you identify covert racism. It's actually quite hard.'
>
> Morgan: 'But Alex, that one is not true.'
>
> Reid: 'But Piers, what you are saying is there are facts and what Alex is saying is there is an experience and perception of those facts which you only appreciate when you are in that situation.'
>
> Morgan: 'On the first part, I agree. If it turns out that a senior member of the royal family, a future king perhaps… who has said this in a derogatory way… that to me would be racism. But the second part of the charge, that Archie has been banned from being a prince because of his skin colour is just untrue. It's nothing to do with racism…'.
>
> Reid: 'But the trouble is she's explaining her experience of it.'
>
> Beresford: 'Exactly, she's explaining her experience of it and do you know what, we've not walked in her shoes.'[40]

The exchange ended up with Morgan walking off and later resigning after being given an ultimatum, amid reports of a complaint made by the Duke and Duchess of Sussex. He has since been vindicated by an Ofcom inquiry.

While there are facts and perceptions of facts, if the latter is wrong, then we should acquiesce and accept we were wrong. What Beresford was arguing for was, in effect, that the testimony of individuals, who in this case likely had an axe to grind, was sufficient to prove the point, prior to any attestation of the facts or right of reply, and even to trump facts when presented. As pointed out in *The Spectator* by

James Innes-Smith, 'lived experience however traumatic, is touted as a form of career currency to put on your CV – just as you would a degree'. He further attributed the development of lived experience as superior knowledge to radical feminists.[41]

What we have is a reasonable concept – first-hand experience that goes by the same name as something else, namely the political idea that perception takes precedence over fact. This is a dangerous idea, in that empirical tests of the claims of demagogues are rendered inadmissible. It is also an idea that suits left-wing radicals who are invariably contradicted by the evidence. Note Althusser's hostility towards empirical social science.

The hegemony of 'lived experience' is further shored up by contemporary radicals. In *Is Everyone Really Equal?* Özlem Sensoy and Robin DiAngelo make the following claims:

> 'Critical theory challenges the claim that any knowledge is neutral or objective, and outside of humanly constructed meanings and interests.
>
> 'There is no neutral text; all texts represent a particular perspective.
>
> 'All texts are embedded with ideology; the ideology embedded in most mainstream texts function to reproduce historical relations of unequal power.'[42]

What such utterances do is preclude the possibility of appeals to evidenced facts as a way of settling political disputes. All that is left is lived experience, only those who make recourse to this argument do not say why their lived experience should trump anyone else's. The only logical destination of this approach is yelling at each other – 'my lived experience!', 'no mine!'.

In any case, the Sewell report *did* account for the 'lived experience' of ethnic minority individuals, through its usage of subjective measures taken from survey data. As pointed out by Robert Tombs, research by the European Union's Agency for Fundamental Human Rights found that perceived discrimination was lowest in the United Kingdom.[43] This research was referenced by Sewell. Moreover, do ethnic minority individuals not have positive 'lived experience', against which the negative might be balanced? Not only does it trump objective fact, bad lived experience is everything, while good lived experience is nowhere.

It can also be added that subjective perception is not necessarily correct. My last report for Civitas found the evidence from the Crime Survey showed that people were prepared to attribute a racial motive to a crime they had been victim of, but when asked why, the reasons were less than convincing. Around 12 per cent of crimes deemed racially-motivated were attributed as such on the grounds that 'some people pick on ethnic minorities'.[44]

'Gaslighting'

'Denying the lived experience' is bad enough, but if you wish to supersede the dogma of racial oppression with a new a narrative emphasising openness and success, despite obvious and glaring problems, then you stand to be accused of 'gaslighting'.

Here is one definition:

> 'Gaslighting is an insidious form of manipulation and psychological control. Victims of gaslighting are deliberately and systematically fed false information that leads them to question what they know to be true, often about themselves. They may end up doubting their memory, their perception, and even their sanity. Over time, a gaslighter's manipulations can grow more complex and potent, making it increasingly difficult for the victim to see the truth.'[45]

The word is taken from the title of a 1938 play 'Gas Light', and subsequent movie, in which a man subtly manipulates a woman into thinking she is going mad in order to have her put in a psychiatric institution because she is unwittingly in possession of evidence of a murder he committed.[46] 'Gaslighting' began as a way to describe abusive men denying to the women they were abusing the truth of what is being done to them. It is a strategy that makes the woman doubt her sanity, and would be cruel as well as manipulative if carried out by any person.

It is a concept that might rightly describe the behaviour of real individuals, both male and female. But it has become increasingly used in politics, and this should not go unchallenged. For example, a letter signed by a group of Labour MPs admonished the Home Secretary Priti Patel for using her 'heritage and experiences of racism to gaslight the very real racism faced by black people and communities across the UK' during a parliamentary debate.[47] Inspection of *Hansard* reveals Patel actually to have acknowledged 'the level of injustice that is felt across the country' and then made reference to her own experiences of racial abuse as evidence she understood racism.[48]

Tony Sewell was not to escape such charges either. Halima Begum of the Runnymede Trust described the Sewell report as 'government-sponsored gaslighting'.[49] Labour MP Dawn Butler referred to 'gaslighting on a national scale'.[50]

Rather than Sewell and his fellow commissioners having studied the facts and consulted widely on them, only to reach a different conclusion from the one Begum and Butler would have liked, it is assumed they have deliberately set out to lie; to damage people mentally, to drive them mad. It is an astonishing charge: not one aimed at the substance of the report but at the intentions of the authors. To suggest that these people did this, nearly all of whom were black or brown, is pretty low.

There is, though, a problem, in that if you have only ever been taught that differences between groups result from white oppression, then the charge appears self-evident. Many people will agree with Begum and Butler.

But many in Soviet Russia also believed they were labouring for the creation of a better society. It was their 'lived experience'. Solzhenitsyn was 'gaslighting' them! When this term becomes legitimate in political discourse, political dissent becomes all the harder. It is granting legitimacy an extreme *ad hominin* attack on reasoned debate. Sewell et al.'s critics might further do well to ask what failing to acknowledge the positives is, if not 'gaslighting' and 'denying the lived experience'. There is not a single germane statistic on the extent of racist violence or racial discrimination that is omitted from Sewell, sufficient to sustain the charge that the issue is being ignored.

Abuse

Commissioner Samir Shah wrote of the vicious backlash he and his colleagues encountered:

> 'The abuse that I and my fellow commissioners received was astonishing. That old racist canard "coconut" was everywhere; we were called "coconut soldiers" (i.e. brown outside, white inside). That was only the mild stuff. The Commission chairman, Tony Sewell, was a particular target: "Tony Sewer", "Tony Sewell is a coon, pass it on", "Sewell Iscariot".'[51]

By rejecting orthodox thought, it is considered they were race traitors, rather than truthful to their own minds. Shah describes their shoddy treatment at the hands of the media:

> 'Many of my fellow commissioners were treated abysmally, forced into rows with antagonists. The BBC tried it on with me too. In an interview on BBC News, the presenter Victoria Derbyshire interrupted to say that the next contributor was early on the line, so would I debate with him/her? I said "no", on the grounds that this was not what we had agreed. I had had no desire to get into a slanging match with anyone.
>
> 'Derbyshire persisted claiming that all of her 'journalistic instincts' told her this was the way to go. I suggested — live on air — that once the interview had concluded she should reflect on her journalistic instincts and question her own ethics.'

He offers a nuanced critique of the fury that ensued, arguing that the 'race-lobby' of which he is a survivor of, being a former chair of the Runnymede Trust, is largely a victim of its own success. The openness in British life to which he testifies did not come about by chance but the result of the industry's efforts. The consequence of this success is organisations like Runnymede become surplus to requirements, and so they need the idea of statistical disparity as necessarily evidence of racism to remain in business. What baffles Shah, however, is the venal conduct of the media with its 'defenestration of impartiality' and barely-concealed desire to stoke rows.

In Plato's analogy of the cave, Socrates tells the story of a group of people who are enslaved within a cave where they work transfixed by shadow puppets, cast against the wall by their captors who remain out of sight. One individual manages to break free and heads out into the light.

There he is at first blinded by it, but gradually his eyes adjust and he comes to realise that the shadows on the wall were not the gods he took them for, and sees them for what they really were. He returns to the cave to try and free his fellows, only to them, he appears to be blind, since his night-vision is now ruined. His extolling of liberty seems like a threat to them, since he has so obviously been harmed by it. So, they kill him as a threat to all that is good and decent. The nefarious ones who cast the shadows do not have to do it. That is the point.

Did Sewell deny the existence of institutional racism?

It was widely reported that the Commission found evidence of racism but no evidence for 'institutional racism'. This though is moot. Consider the following from *The Guardian*:

> 'It [the Sewell report] concluded the "claim the country is still institutionally racist is not borne out by the evidence"'.[52]

That sentence appears nowhere in the Sewell report proper, but is instead taken from the accompanying press briefing which said:

> 'The well-meaning idealism of many young people who claim the country is still institutionally racist is not borne out by the evidence...'.[53]

It is fair to report a government press release. It is also fair to quote an interview with Sewell in which he says, '... evidence of actual institutional racism? No, that wasn't there, we didn't find that in our report'.[54] But this was not mentioned in the actual report.

Sewell further said in the same interview:

> 'What we have seen is the term institutional racism is sometimes wrongly applied and it's a sort of catch-all phrase for microaggressions or acts of racial abuse.'[55]

This is interesting and indeed true. Consider the following extracts from an interview with Parm Sandhu, who is a former chief superintendent at the Metropolitan Police and has appeared on Channel 4's *Murder Island*:

> 'It would be wrong for me to comment on the authors or the credibility of that report, but it's not a reflection of my lived experiences. They [Sewell's commission] could have spoken to me. I could have guided them because living through my experience... institutional racism exists in the Met Police. So if it exists in the Met Police, it exists in other large organisations...'.

Again, the insistence of the power of the 'lived experience' of an individual as conclusive proof of the condition of an institution. But the only examples given in the interview are of abuse experienced in the course of her duties, presumably by members of the public and not the police:

> 'People are saying go home. Where do families like mine go home to[?] Because we were all born in this country, our grandparents and parents were all from different countries, Jamaica, China, India, where would they like us to be repatriated to other than to Handsworth in Birmingham?'[56]

Further note that the Sewell report has a section on the abuse of police officers, with a focus on how minority officers are racially abused, and often by people of ethnic minorities who see them as traitors. Racial abuse, including violent assaults of police officers, spiked during the Black Lives Matter protests of 2020 in London. This will be inevitable when people in positions of authority persist in saying the police are racist.

The Sewell report attempts to reign in the definitional laxity by proposing the following definition of institutional racism:

> 'Applicable to an institution that is racist or to the discriminatory processes, policies, attitudes of behaviours in a single institution.'

Compare this with the definition of the Macpherson report.

Note the differences while also the contradiction of Sewell that it believes it to have 'stood the test of time':

> 'The collective failure of an organisation to provide an appropriate and professional service to people because of their colour, culture, or ethnic origin. It can be seen or detected in processes, attitudes and behaviour which amount to discrimination through unwitting prejudice, ignorance, thoughtlessness and racist stereotyping which disadvantage minority ethnic people.'

It should be added that the Macpherson definition was an innovation in itself, distinct from that used in the Scarman report into rioting in Brixton. Its author Lord Scarman actually had two definitions which he could not decide between:

> 'If, by [institutionally racist] it is meant that it [Britain] is a society which knowingly, as a matter of policy, discriminates against black people, I reject the allegation. If, however, the suggestion being made is that practices may be adopted by public bodies as well as private individuals which are unwittingly discriminatory against black people, then this is an allegation which deserves serious consideration, and, where proved, swift remedy.'[57]

Macpherson's redefinition, to expunge the 'matter of policy' test, allowed him to reach his conclusion of institutional racism in the Metropolitan police, since he found no evidence of any racist policies. More widely, the concept of institutional racism is not nailed down, nor is their consensus among academic scholars as to what it means. In 1983, John Solomons described it as a 'catch-all phrase' to describe all forms of racial discrimination.[58] This predates Macpherson and utilises the exact same words used by Sewell nearly 40 years later.

The Macpherson report distinguished between personal racism and institutional racism. The former was defined in terms of 'conduct or words or practices' that 'advantage or disadvantage people because of their colour, culture or ethnic origin'. What Sandhu complained of would surely fall under such terms.

The problem with the Macpherson definition lies in that it seeks to define a property of institutions, without adequately defining what institutions are. Then it says whatever this property is, it is made manifest in the behaviour of individuals. If every individual in a given institution meets the definition of Macpherson's 'racism', then that would be sufficient evidence of institutional racism. Macpherson's definition of institutional racism thus encompasses both the racism of individuals and something else – the failure to provide an appropriate service, only we are told nothing of what this might be or how it is distinctly made manifest.

The problem is compounded by the excess use of words and ideas that require explication themselves – what is a 'collective failure', for instance, when it is possible in any institution some individuals behave well while others badly? What are an 'appropriate service' and 'unwitting prejudice'?

While critics are correct in that this concept is nebulous and empirically unmeasurable, it is not true to say that it cannot exist. Sewell is correct in his attempt to nail it down.

In order to provide a definition for this concept of 'institutional racism', it is necessary to delve into the conceptual academic literature on institutions. Ironically, it is also nebulous. One paper by Claudius Graebner and Amineh Ghorbani reviews the varying usage of the term 'institution' in economics. It proposes all definitions share at heart the idea of 'codifiable systems of social structures (in particular norms and rules) that lead to inclinations for people to act in specific ways'.[59]

Such a definition does not mandate that such institutional rules necessarily lead to behaviour. This is important, and a point which I will return to. But first it is pointed out that the Macpherson report found no evidence of any explicitly racist policy within the Metropolitan Police. Moreover, the Public Sector Equality Duty of the Equality Act 2010 mandates all public authorities 'eliminate discrimination' and 'advance equality of opportunity'. All public institutions are arguably not institutionally racist since it is written into their rules that they promote equality between groups. Moreover, it is against the law to discriminate, yet individuals may still contravene such institutional rules.[60]

Institutional racism is when racist ideas, inequality of worth between the races or ethnic groups, is at the heart of the rules that form a particular institution. It should be pointed out that Graebner and Ghorbani's definition depends on the word 'codifiable', and that individuals can rebel against institutional rules.

It is possible that we have *de facto* institutional racism within institutions in the United Kingdom. Evidence for that would not be the presence of discrimination in hiring, for example, but for the tolerance of discrimination in hiring. CV-tests, or correspondence studies as they are known, only provide evidence of the former. Moreover, since there is *de jure* institutional equality – as evidenced by the Public Sector Equality Duty of the Equality Act 2010 – whatever *de facto* institutional racism there might be, it can always be cowed due to the existence of formal legal remedy. To be clear, this is not to rule out the possibility of racist actors and behaviour within any given institution, but rather to offer a way of thinking that distinguishes between properties of institutions and those of individuals.

The practice of ethnic discrimination, as well as religious and caste, have been demonstrated to exist in countries all over the world, including majority non-white ones such as India, Malaysia and China. One academic review found CV-tests were largely the preserve of Western countries, with only a handful of studies carried out elsewhere.[61]

The concern with discrimination here, that borders on obsession, is not shared globally, although the behaviour is. Routinely, we reach for such studies to prove the failings of white people and, somehow, institutions. No studies have been attempted to test whether or not, say, the Pakistani proprietor, thriving in Britain, has ethnic preferences too in hiring. Discrimination is assumed to be the bad behaviour of white people.

If this is a global and common behaviour, then surely this is to do with group membership. Ethnic Chinese people are discriminated against in the United Kingdom as well as Malaysia. Despite this, they show positive disparate outcomes in both countries. However, in China, they discriminate against Uighur Muslims. These relationships have all been confirmed empirically.

If these individuals stayed in China, they would not experience discrimination, nor would they experience the benefits of living outside China, namely greater prosperity and political freedom. There is a trade-off between the benefits of belonging to the ethnic majority and living in freer and more prosperous societies. The benefits can be empirically demonstrated by statistics on longevity – see Chapter 3. Yet, none of this is ever factored in to our appraisal of British openness and the experience of ethnic minority groups. It is only ever a question of wickedness that is to be corrected by a radical seizing of power.

Such CV-studies may also be taken to mean the problem is 'systemic', that this pertains, somehow, to the system. This argument was made by Sunder Katwala at an event hosted by Policy Exchange.[62] However, what precisely this has to do with the system is not clear, either in this country or in other countries such as Mexico, China, India and Peru, where the same method has been applied.[63] Nor is it clear how this cannot be seen as a property of individuals, not systems, namely the common homophilic preference for people who are similar. Given that we have this phenomenon occurring in countries with different histories and institutions – different systems – this would seem the more likely attribution.

Peoples can be horrible to each other the world over. It is neither new, nor unique to white people. Yet we favour a 'zero racism' approach which demands that *very human* behaviours should *never occur*, not just that they are wrong.

The Portes critique

Jonathan Portes, writing in *The Byline Times*, complained that the Sewell report precluded the possibility of finding evidence of institutional racism or racism as causal in explaining ethnic disparity. He points to a section in the Sewell report where definitions are offered for 'explained' and 'unexplained disparities':

> 'Explained racial disparities: this term should be used when there are persistent ethnic differential outcomes that can demonstrably be shown to be a result of other factors such as geography, class or sex.
>
> 'Unexplained racial disparities: persistent differential outcomes for ethnic groups with no conclusive evidence

> about the causes. This applies to situations where a disparate outcome is identified, but there is no evidence as to what is causing it.'[64]

Portes writes:

> 'So disparities are either explained by factors other than racism – or there is no evidence so they are unexplained. Thus, apparently, while racism does exist... there is no way, within its framework, to demonstrate, through the use of evidence or analysis, that racism or discrimination, indirect or direct, is actually causing the observed disparities in outcomes.
>
> 'Therefore, it is not that the Commission did not find any evidence that disparities are the result of race or racism – it excluded the possibility *ex ante*.'

The mistake Portes makes is to take these words out of context, pick a logical flaw, and then to overstate their significance. They came from a section in the report on how we might succinctly define concepts such as 'institutional racism' to help focus debate, to avoid talking at cross purposes and to reign in semantic inflation. It does not follow that this provided some sort of standard by which the Commission weighed up evidence.

He further criticises the section of the report on the labour market – 'my specialist area'. He complains that the report indulges in some 'fairly crude sleight of hand', in other words, deliberate distortion. But his argument is wrong in that he claims Sewell only managed to claim convergence in employment based on unadjusted employment rates, 'presumably because adjustment would increase the size of the gaps'. This is assuming bad faith without evidence.

He disputes the claim that CV-tests for discrimination – correspondence studies – prove the existence of discrimination but 'cannot be relied upon to provide clarity on the extent that it happens in everyday life'. Portes writes, 'nobody who has actually read or understood the research could have written this'. In fact, Sewell is correct.

As I argued elsewhere, there is a distinction in research design between internal and external validity. The former pertains to the extent the design is a fair test, the latter the extent to which the findings can be generalised to the wider population.[65] Since correspondence studies rely not on random sampling but whatever data comes to the researcher, they cannot be generalised – the external validity is too low. Thus, claims of ethnic minority individuals having to send 60 per cent more applications in order to get a call back for an interview are invalid. That is simply an experimental finding.

Portes cites Manning and Rose's critique as well as Marmot's, which were addressed above and found wanting. Indeed, he cites other critics with 'acknowledged expertise' who he presents as delivering knockout blows.[66]

That would be to flatter them – sometimes they land their target, but mostly not. Take criminologist Alex Stevens' critique, posted on Twitter, where he rightly points to some selective quoting from a study of stop and search.[67] But he further accuses the report of misrepresenting the Angiolini review (it does not) and he complains, the 'Commission write that age and deprivation explains much of the difference between ethnic groups. The cited report actually shows the disparity is not washed away by deprivation'. But in what way is the first sentence incompatible with the second? Moreover, Portes references Kenan Malik as an authority on 'family structure' when he is not and his critique barely scratches on that issue.[68]

All research can be criticised, there is usually a flaw somewhere. A report written by multiple authors, working remotely due to lockdown, will be especially vulnerable. But claiming decisive victories where there are none is disingenuous.

Portes writes that in his 35-year-long career he has never seen a report where 'the evidence and analysis has [sic] been so comprehensively dismantled so quickly and completely'. As I have shown, the critics at best can point to some flaws, but for the most part, their criticism could be rebutted or mitigated on reasonable grounds. Portes' own arguments, as well as those he references made by others, are by no means decisive.

Another prominent criticism of the report was that it was mistaken in its methodology, in that it sought to explain away differences between ethnic groups by attributing them to other factors. The argument is that the report showed a given ethnic disparity was not really a difference between ethnic groups, but rather a spurious correlation, and really an effect of something like social class. Therefore, the argument goes, Sewell concluded that it was not racism because there were no differences between ethnic groups. This though would be an error in that racism causes poverty, which leads to disparate outcomes. The two cannot be separated statistically.

This argument can be attributed to Jonathan Portes, who wrote of 'a basic statistical error' which 'every undergraduate learning about quantitative methods in social science should recognise'.[69]

There are two objections to this argument. The first is that the Sewell report does not chiefly rely on such reasoning. The second is that even if it did, even if Sewell had produced a regression model which showed all ethnic differences became null once a measure of socioeconomic status was introduced, critics such as Portes would have to explain why this showed that within social classes, ethnic minority individuals were having equal outcomes with white ones, as that is what the regression model would be telling you. That would not be consistent with the expectations of a 'structurally racist' society.

What was the actual method used for explaining disparity?

If the Sewell report is to be criticised, it is in that it never makes explicit what its standards are for explaining a 'disparity' on any given measure between ethnic groups. The Sewell report was presented as being a continuation of the approach begun under May, in that first the data were gathered and published to be explained later, and then policies proposed. The only significant difference was that the personnel switched from May to Johnson and Woolley to Sewell in the meantime.

What persisted was a lack of explication as to what constitutes 'explanation'. However, reading the report, you find implicit another method, namely something akin to 'natural experiments'.

Experiments in science are when all other factors are held constant so that the effect of a treatment can be established. Natural experiments are when you have circumstances whereby groups present themselves as similar, so much so that causal inference may be possible. The most prominent example of this is in the section on educational performance where it is noted that black Caribbean children do worse than white British children on some measures, notably school exclusions. However, black African children do considerably better here, and given that they are also black and have comparable socioeconomic backgrounds, as well as likely equal exposure to racism, racism cannot be said to the causal factor.

Notably, the differences between ethnic groups are those that persist after regression analysis, with the data taken from the Timpson Review and presented in the graph below. That is to say, causal inference was not contingent on explaining away correlations.

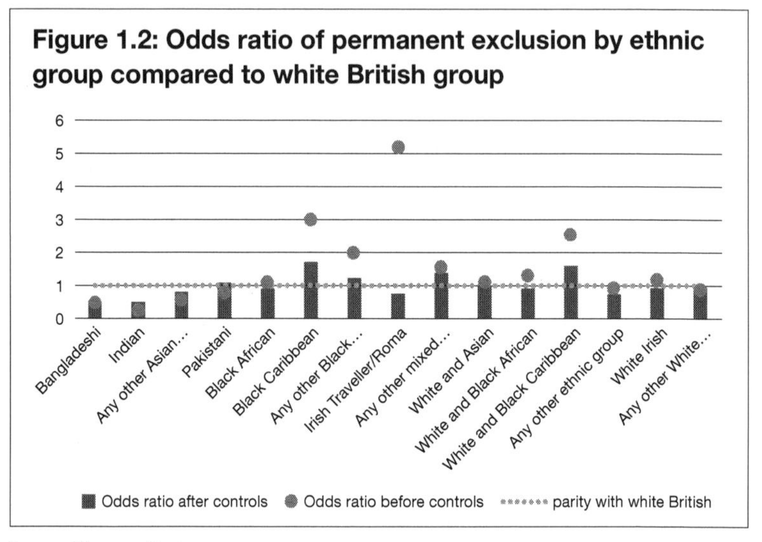

Figure 1.2: Odds ratio of permanent exclusion by ethnic group compared to white British group

Source: Timpson Review.

Other times, the Sewell report rests on arguments by recourse to authority, resting on the citation of independent experts. While they may be correct, we are only presented with the citation and not the method. One example of this would be to *support* the contention that racism causes disparate risk of psychosis and depression among black people, through citing a report by Professor Kamaldeep Bhui of Queen Mary University of London. This though is undermined, largely through Sewell's referencing of comparable elevated risks for white immigrants in majority white countries.

Elsewhere, in reference to Covid-19, it is concluded that the elevated risk for minority individuals can be in part attributed to population density, socio-demographics, and greater comorbidity such as obesity, diabetes, and chronic kidney disease. However, the report does not comment on the data it presents showing an elevated risk for black and Asian people in Wave 1 of the pandemic (January – August 2020), but just for Asian people in Wave 2 (September – December 2020).[70]

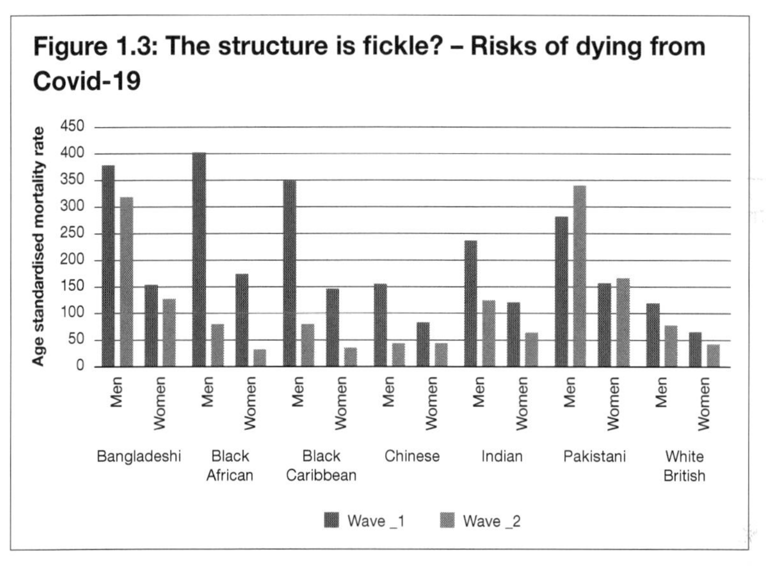

Figure 1.3: The structure is fickle? – Risks of dying from Covid-19

Source: Commission on Racial and Ethnic Disparities.

Generally, though, the section on health rests on the observation that ethnic minority people tend to have better health than white people, overall and in pre-pandemic 'normal' conditions. This is not consistent with the image of a 'structure' that is out to get ethnic minorities. The report then tries to link differences in outcome in part to genetic differences and in part to socioeconomic factors. Largely, though, it fails to reach any definite conclusions, primarily because ethnic minority groups often tend to have lower levels of wealth and higher rates of poverty. The pattern does not hold up. It is a mystery. This is, in part, why further research is called for in this area.

One of the few passages where racism is explicitly raised as explanans is in the section on healthcare. Data on patient satisfaction are presented to show overall scant difference between groups, but that Asian groups tended to report lower satisfaction with GP services:

> 'It is important to note that majorities of all groups report positive experiences and that while the relative lack of satisfaction with GP services among some British Asian people is of concern, the overall picture suggests that racism and discrimination are not widespread in the health system, as is sometimes claimed, as black groups are more or less equal in their satisfaction to white groups.'

In other words, a racist healthcare system is unlikely to produce content black people, to the same degree as white people. In short, it is all about the inability to evidence consistency of worse outcomes which would be expected under structural racism. Simply, the data are too varied with all manner of groups from comparable backgrounds, equally exposed to racism, having sometimes better, sometimes worse, sometimes the same outcomes. Needless to say, the data on NHS satisfaction are the 'lived experience' of ethnic minority individuals.

A break from past reports?

There is a compelling critique to be made of the Sewell report (see below), but it was not made by the great and good. Mostly, they were wide of the mark. Moreover, I have read all the recent reviews on race and was able to find substantial problems with all of them. The McGregor-Smith Review, for example, had its limitations too, yet there are few critiques save mine.[71] The question then, is how come the Sewell report drew such fire and fury?

In the aftermath of Sewell, we have seen presented by the criticism, for example by the Runnymede Trust, that the Sewell report is a distraction and deviation from all the other past reviews that contain supposedly all this knowledge about how to end racism and bring about an equality of outcomes. But the government has sat upon this knowledge and done nothing. There are good, moral reviews, and then there is Tony Sewell's naughty review.

This is disingenuous. Firstly, all the past reviews contained simply suggestions of what should be done by individuals outside of government, not commitments made by it. By my reckoning, of the 35 recommendations made by the Lammy Review, 26 were (or are being) directly implemented, with five partially so, two rejected, and a further two were compensated for by something else in the spirit of the initial recommendation.[72]

According to a Ministry of Justice document:

> 'There is now a wide-ranging programme of work in place – both responding to the 35 specific recommendations made by David Lammy MP and work taking the agenda above and beyond this.'[73]

It went on to say it had invited Lammy to inspect the Ministry of Justice's efforts and that he had then given evidence to a House of Commons select committee:

> 'Lammy recognised significant positive activity as a result of the review and was pleased in regard to the governance structure that has been established to progress the recommendations in his review.'

Perhaps one day Conservative politicians will come to reflect on the wisdom of asking a Labour MP to come up with policies for them. In any case, some recommendations found within this body of policy literature will obviously not work in reducing racial disparity. For example, the Timpson Review of school expulsions recommended to make teachers more ethnically diverse. Given that school expulsions are rare for some minority groups, for whom teachers are just as ethnically diverse as for the one group for which it is a notable problem – black Caribbean – it is obvious that greater diversity will not change a thing. Crucially, black African children are just as likely to be expelled as comparable white British children.

Moreover, the McGregor-Smith Review's recommendation to introduce mandatory unconscious bias training for all employees would have cost at least £915 million.[74] This intervention has been shown to be, at best, highly dubious.[75]

It should also be added that the Lammy Review mentioned 'structural racism' precisely *zero* times. The same was true of the Timpson Review. The Williams Review into the 'Windrush Scandal' was 'unable to make a definitive finding of institutional racism', finding only 'elements'. These elements amounted to a lack of awareness about race, with senior government figures demonstrating 'little awareness of indirect discrimination nor the way in which race, immigration and nationality intersect'.

Other elements of institutional racism, found by Wendy Williams, were high levels of ethnic diversity towards the bottom of the Home Office, but low at the top, while take up of diversity and unconscious bias training was low. I only need point out that the Home Office has offices in Croydon, meaning its clerical and administrative roles will be filled often by local people, ensuring high diversity, while the top of the Home Office is ethnically diverse in line with the share of minority individuals who entered the Civil Service Fast Stream in the early 2000s – seven per cent.

But why were these reviews not pilloried for denying 'lived experience'?

Critiquing Sewell

Tony Sewell's commission was radical in that it proved itself savvy to Thomas Sowell's 'invincible fallacy'.

This is the idea that differences between groups are necessarily caused by one group oppressing the other. But concomitant to this in Sowell's writing is the common attestation that government has any particular competency in correcting disparity between groups. That government has the moral right to intervene to correct differences, that if not stemming from racism, may stem from differences in freely chosen behaviours, is also a questionable assertion. In this line, Sewell's commission is orthodox.

For all the furore over the report, the very same critics sometimes tended to be supportive of the recommendations made. See, for instance, the critiques of Jonathan Portes, Kenan Malik, and the British Medical Association (BMA).

The BMA declared itself, despite its deep reservations, supportive of recommendations made by Sewell, including '[t]he call for the establishment of an Office for Health Disparities'.[76] According to the Sewell report, this would be 'an independent body which would work alongside the NHS, as part of, or in place of, the redesigned Public Health England'. We are told, since most 'health inequalities' are not down to 'differences in healthcare, addressing them will involve multiple government departments and so the office would need to be cross-cutting across government'.

Its functions would include:

(a) 'Increasing programmes aimed at levelling up health care and health outcomes', using 'existing data and evidence to target those communities with the worst health outcomes... for tailored health interventions, health education and communications'.

(b) 'Improving the data, guidance and expertise in the causes and solutions for health disparities for specific groups.'

But data improvements and better targeting were supposed to be the preserve of the Cabinet Office's Race Disparity Unit. The proposed Office for Health Disparities largely seems intended to produce more research and increase public awareness.

Sewell continues:

> 'Establish a team of experts with cultural understanding of different communities, including white groups, to provide nationwide advice to health care providers.'

Such direction is fairly common and could have been taken from any other government review into ethnic disparity, or the Runnymede Trust report for that matter. While the BMA welcomed such a recommendation, it pointed out that an organisation similar to the proposed Office for Health Disparities already exists, namely the Race and Health Observatory. That is part of the NHS and, according to its own website, exists to 'identify and tackle ethnic inequalities in health and care by facilitating research, making health policy recommendations and enabling long-term transformational change'.[77] But instead of saying 'no thanks, we've already got one', the BMA simply asks for clarification of the intended purpose.

Going back to the Sewell report, recall that it stated the Office would work 'as part of, or in place of' Public Health England, which is being 'redesigned'. If it is being 'redesigned', having only begun operating in 2013, then this means its initial design was botched. Yet we are asked to believe that the same types of people, often the very same individuals, can come up with a new design to solve problems we apparently still do not adequately understand. This is evident in Sewell's stipulation that so much of the proposed Office would be concerned with yet more research.

Regarding liberty, if one thing has become apparent during the course of the pandemic, it is that *health is power*. In Scotland, Nicola Sturgeon has been granted control over matters of basic freedom, including the power to prevent people from Manchester coming to Scotland, on the proviso that she guarantees the nation's health. This was never the intention of the policy of devolution.

The Sewell proposal for an Office of Health Disparities seems like the nod for the usual suspects to further occupy the ministries of state in order that they might make people be healthy. Indeed, an Office for Health Improvement and Disparities has since been created, coming into existence in September 2021. Judging by its early communications, it appears to be a continuation of the approach taken by Public Health England of trying to reduce obesity, smoking, and drinking.[78]

Note that knife crime is now a 'public health' concern, with violence seen as 'a preventable disease'. The BMA welcomed Sewell's 'call for an evidence-based pilot that diverts offences of low-level Class B drug possession into public health services' and supports a 'health in all policies approach'.[79] This sets out the scope of the ambition, with the vested interests behind state healthcare looking to colonise evermore fields of social life.

But if you carry a knife or take drugs, you are not ill. You are breaking the law. If you are ill, you are largely not responsible for your condition, unless you have engaged in risky behaviours that were causal. Pushing crime into the realm of healthcare only serves to diminish the responsibility, necessary to get people to stop these destructive behaviours. If you are ill, you are excused responsibility and permitted to lie in bed rather than go out to work. If you are immoral, you are asked to change your ways or face sanctions.

It is clear that 'public health' means much more than what is immediately evident, with a definition inferred from its usage to mean the state taking a greater role in the lives of supposedly free individuals.

Of those 'experts with cultural understanding of different communities', it can be pointed out that what they have to offer is of little use. At best, these people study patterns of correlation at the aggregate level of groups. They try and account for correlations with other variables, using the techniques of statistical analysis, such as regression. However, groups do not present themselves in the doctor's surgery or at the hospital. This is because doctors and nurses treat individuals. Information as to what is causing the patient's complaints is garnered through clinical examination of individuals, not statistical analyses of groups.

Moreover, such statistical approaches usually seem to be about trying to find the cause of any given outcome by looking at correlations with other outcomes. A key past event will likely not feature in any cross-sectional snapshot of an individual's life.

Sewell said in a speech defending his report, given to Policy Exchange:

> 'Our recommendations provide much of the prose for a new, open-minded, proudly multi-ethnic chapter of the British story. One that doesn't shy away from what more needs to

be done to address racial inequalities, this is by no way a finished project, what we have done here is given a number of recommendations to significantly move this forward.'[80]

In truth, these are recommendations made by individuals that they believe will work, but without any evidence that they will. The proof will be in the pudding, when its burden ought to be on those making the recommendation.

Family structure

A key variable in explaining racial disparity is what Sewell calls 'family structure', to mean a continuum from the nuclear family to what might be called the sub-atomic family, composed of single, never-married parents who live remotely and pursue their own pleasures. No numbers are crunched to show how once you account for family structure, the differences abate.

Rather a pattern is noticed whereby those groups that tend to do worse – black and poor whites – have high levels of family breakdown, high levels of criminality and low levels of educational attainment. These are not issues impacting on Asian families to the same degree, which are built much more on traditional cultural and religious reserve. Statistics are presented to show that 63 per cent of black Caribbean children were growing up in lone parent families, and 43 per cent of black African. This compares to Indian children at six per cent.[81] Research is further cited linking father absence to 'children's worse educational performance, emotional development, and adult mental health', as well as 'increased likelihood of youth incarceration'.

These data can be supplemented with data on marriage rates and children in care. Around 47 per cent of Asian households are formed by a married couple, as are 32.9 per cent of white households. For black households, the figure is

21.6 per cent. By contrast, 24.3 per cent of black households are lone parent, compared to 8.8 per cent of Asian and 10.2 per cent of white.[82] There are about 80,000 children in care in England, as of 2020, of which seven per cent are black and four per cent are Asian. These compare respectively with five and 10 per cent of children overall (those aged 0-18).[83]

The report further notes that this far better matches the data than explanations to do with poverty, since many ethnic groups experience this more but have better outcomes. This is not the same as the 'regression method' outlined by critics such as Portes.

It is a credible explanation, only missing is precisely why this matters. Sewell points out that single parent families may offer an equally nurturing environment, but pins their greater likelihood of failure on the idea of two parents being better than one. This though misses the obvious truth that children who commit serious violent crime have a moral failing, and this will be brought on by their being insufficiently integrated into society. The lack of a father entails either the lack of a disciplinarian or the mother being overworked to the point of being too tired to provide sufficient moral grounding.

The Sewell report speaks of a 'welcome' revolution in family structure, only 'as these freedoms have grown, there is also greater stress on families and the prevalence of breakdown has increased'. This though would ignore the rising fortunes of all, including ethnic minorities, as evidenced by their growing share of the middle-class, and declining racial hostility (see Chapter 3). It would seem there is less financial stress on families and greater freedom to live apart.

Statistics show that in the 1970s, at a time when racism was much more prevalent than today, the black family was in much better health. According to the Policy Studies Institute, in 1974, 13 per cent of black Caribbean families with children were lone parent. By 1994, it had risen to between 36 and 45 per cent, depending on the definition used. Since then, the share has remained broadly stable. At the same time, the black Caribbean middle-class has grown, implying rising prosperity.[84]

Critics such as Theodore Dalrymple and Thomas Sowell point to a welfare state mentality, whereby the good intentions behind it engender perverse incentives that become morally corrupting. Rather than work to provide for your child, you can pursue gratification of your own desires, leaving the state to provide instead. The Sewell report is aware of these ideas, speaking of a 'cultural change relating to male responsibility, the welfare state and growing affluence making it possible to bring up children alone'. But in response, what it proposes is more state 'support' to families – without realising this may further extend those very same perverse incentives.

Alexander Adams wrote in *The Critic* lately:

> 'In the 1940s, political theorist James Burnham set out the idea of a managerial elite. He stated that an elite class of bureaucrats and managers would create a technocracy by eroding the authority of the Church, community and family, undercutting capitalist entrepreneurs through regulation and bypassing electoral democracy. This seems to have come to pass.'[85]

The support proposed in the Sewell report risks following on in this vein, whereby rather than build resilience within families, as is the stated intention, you build dependency for what should come naturally, from generation to generation, namely the knowledge of how to be a good parent.

But first, the state technocrats need to find this out for themselves, since more 'data about family strain' and 'academic research into cultural attitudes and parenting styles' are called for. This is all part of a proposed 'Support for Families' review which should 'develop a series of actions' for:

- Better in-school 'support' services for parents, including 'school-parent contracts' to build 'relations between schools and parents';
- More flexible working for single parents;
- More involvement for parents in dealings with the police concerning youth crime; and
- More family therapy and 'group support' where families break down.

All this would seem to have the potential to serve to make it easier for families to break down, while increasing the bond not within families but between individual and the state. This project is to involve Dame Rachel de Souza, who is Children's Commissioner of England. She cannot make you stay with your wife and children. Nor is the secret to family success a secret. You sacrifice, you provide, you be there, you cooperate and compromise for the good of the children. It does not require Dame Rachel to figure it out.

We have seen these reviews many times before. Did Dame Louise Casey solve our integration problems? The Children's Commissioner's Office has recently, we are told, launched a survey of children called 'the Big Ask'. When adults ask children what to do, they have given up any claim to authority, and can expect only to be told things along the lines of we need to save the planet and eat more ice cream in return. All too often, we have this expectation that children, in their state of innocence, will come up with solutions to our problems. But what will this be grounded on? Their wealth of experience, or perhaps, realistic expectations?

We further know that 'support' is already available in the form of state benefits, particularly child benefit. As seen in the graph below, claims for this form of 'support' are roughly as high among black, Pakistani and Bangladeshi families, but the children growing up in single parent families is pronounced only among black people.[86] Clearly, 'support' does not buy you fathers.

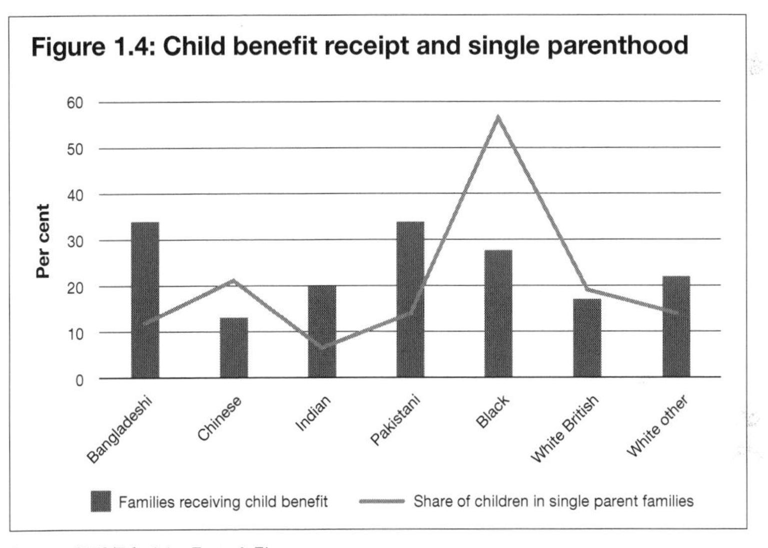

Source: ONS/Ethnicity Facts & Figures.

As an early indicator of the impact of the Sewell report, the government has announced £500 million to 'support' families, including £80 million to create 75 'family hubs', an idea endorsed by Sewell. £100 million will be spent on 'the mental health of expectant parents', with £120 million on 'other comprehensive family support programmes'. £200 million will be spent on 300,000 individuals deemed 'most vulnerable'. These are eye-watering sums of money, but were immediately denounced as 'not enough' by charities and opposition political parties. What exactly is being bought by this money is unclear, nor what the ethos of these programmes are. Is the state building family resilience or indulging its destruction, fostering dependency and replacing folk knowledge of parenting with state technocracy?[87]

Ethos and agency

If we look at educational performance judged by Progress 8 scores, a measure of pupil progress made against a national average, then we see that while black performance may be poor in part, some of the best performing black children are to be found in Islamic schools.[88]

Given that Bangladeshi and Pakistani people are mostly Muslim, and given black Muslim children do well in school, it would suggest this is not a matter of state support, but rather one of ethos. Note also that black boys sometimes do better in local authority areas where they are fewer in number – see the difference in performance between black boys in Newcastle and those in Lambeth in the graph below. The most able who attend selective schools have no problem at all, they actively thrive, while those in the state-funded mainstream do much worse. Importantly, black boys in selective schools outperform white boys in selective schools by a factor of around 1.7.[89]

All this would suggest educational success is to do with drive fulfilled within areas where there are clear social rules; and that failure is a result of social *anomie* (discussed in Chapter 6). The Sewell report rightly sees there is a problem but risks setting in motion bureaucratic interventions that will not resolve it. It seeks to manufacture agency rather than appeal to it.

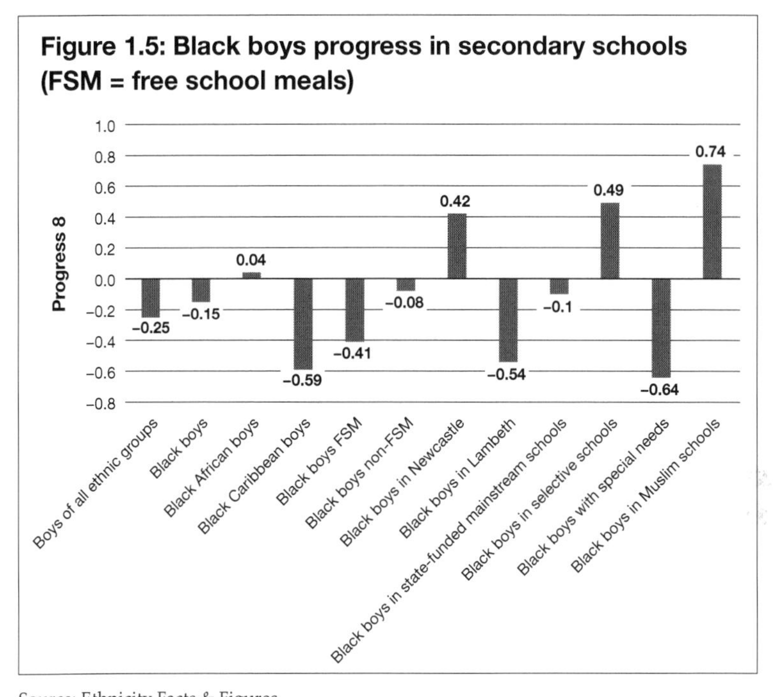

Figure 1.5: Black boys progress in secondary schools (FSM = free school meals)

Source: Ethnicity Facts & Figures.

The act of manufacturing appeals to the interests of the manufacturer, while the promised joys are by no means assured. During the Black Lives Matter protests of 2020 in London, the actor John Boyega gave an impassioned speech. It was in marked contrast to the usual narratives of the Black Lives Matter movement in that he took specific issue with the behaviour of black men. Here is an extract:

> 'They want us to be disorganised, but not today. Not today. Not today. This message is specifically for black men. Black men, black men, we need to take care of our black women. We need to [take] care of them. They are us. They are us. They are our future. We cannot demonise our own.
>
> 'We are the pillars of the family. Imagine this, a nation that is set up with individual families that are thriving, that are healthy, that communicate, that raise their children in love.

> 'Have a better rate of becoming better human beings. And that's what we need to create. Black men, it starts with you.'[90]

His speech was emotional, and no more so than when he spoke the above words. Was this not an appeal to agency, for black men to be better husbands and fathers? And how come this was so well received by the Black Lives Matter audience whose usual fare is racist police, disparity and 'the system'?

Black London is far removed from my experience, despite my having lived in Peckham, where Boyega is from. But you do catch glimpses of the deep pain among those men and women who have grown up without their fathers. The only real solution to this is for such fathers not to do it anymore. It takes a decision that is not the gift of civil servants. Boyega's approach of trying to inspire better behaviour may have much greater chance of success than technocratic approaches that might be dreamed up from within Whitehall.

Money

The most vehement critics of the Sewell report often have links to organisations that advocate diversity and inclusion, or campaign against racism. For such organisations, disparate outcomes are both evidence of systemic or institutional racism and caused by them. That this is tautological is neither here nor there.

The Sewell report represented a direct threat to them for the following reasons:

1. Disparate outcomes are caused by things other than racism and therefore anti-racist organisations offer little of value, so why go back to them for more?
2. It is highly sceptical about the value of diversity and inclusion schemes, noting that they seldom work, may backfire, and are 'not standardised or certified'.

3. Its rejection of the *cause celebre,* mandatory ethnicity pay gap reporting, which would have, if enacted, provided diversity and inclusion/anti-racism organisations with ample ground for work without end.

While the vested interest is often obvious, it should be added that many did not realise that Sewell still offered them the chance to reconvene, to continue to practice their dubious trade. It does nothing to challenge the validity of the idea of the pay gap as a problem, since it calls for further research and remedy where necessary. It calls for smarter interventions to mediate conflicts within the workplace and so on, while the proposed Office for Health Disparities and increased funding for the Equality and Human Rights Commission (EHRC) should have had them licking their lips.

Diversity and inclusion, and anti-racism are big business, while Black Lives Matter, which purports to be anti-capitalist, has been a gold rush. In the United States, funding from charitable foundations and donors for organisations concerned with racial equality amounted to $4.2 billion for the *first half of* 2020. That was *20 per cent more* than for 2011-19 combined.[91]

Here in the United Kingdom, a report by *The Funders for Race Equality Alliance* found that charitable foundations and funders made available £106 million during the early stages of the Covid-19 pandemic, of which £47 million (44.5 per cent) went to 'black and minority ethnic voluntary and community organisations'.[92] It is hard to say how much direct support comes from the state, and this should be an object of future research.

The Sewell report was denounced by a coalition of 62 charitable foundations, including the Barrow Cadbury Trust, Comic Relief, and Paul Hamlyn Foundation. This took the form of an open letter to Boris Johnson, which took issue with the 'report's downplaying of the impact of racism and comments from [Sewell] that the review did not find actual evidence of institutional racism', and that 'our partners and communities who face racism have been unduly dismissed and their lived experiences denied…'.[93]

Again, 'lived experience'. The letter does not actually point to anywhere in the report where a factual error has been made or one of inference, nor the many examples of survey data that look to capture the 'lived experience' of individuals. It is in effect a demand that Sewell's conclusions match the complaints of those who complain most prominently. The signatories call for Johnson to distance himself from 'narratives that deny the harm caused by racism in our society', while they profess themselves committed and pure of heart – in that they 'remain resolute and continue to drive towards a just society'. They are also at pains to stress their own faults, decrying 'inequitable power structures' and that 'we have not always got this right'.

The problem with this letter is most of the major private backers of research are declaring findings on race that defy their expectation to be *anathema*. The cost to this is that the sceptical voice that points to the mistakes of orthodoxy and group think is lost, ruled invalid *ex ante*. This is the price paid for the signatories to show their virtue, who, judging by their names and positions, are largely white and likely very well off.

Revealing is one article by Naima Khan, who is director of the Inclusive Mosque Initiative as well as having had a career in the charity sector. In an article on the Sewell report, specifically addressed to charitable funders, she speaks of a 'gaslighting crisis'. The problem is, she writes, the Sewell report 'now further legitimates' describing anti-racist campaigners as lobbying groups who rely on 'lived experience'. These are actually noble organisations that are relaying vital evidence of oppression, or so she argues. Khan's main concern, however, is that 'funders aren't attuned to how they too participate in gaslighting'.[94] She urges funders to speak the language of grievance, to use 'terms like injustice and "systemic oppression"'. As she puts it, 'often charities will adapt their language to that of the funder'. She continues, 'Some funders already happily acknowledge sexism, transphobia, ableism etc. and this practice supports charities and activists working for long-term change to access funding and achieve their goals.' It seems like an Orwellian attempt to control the language in order to dictate the outcome, namely money directed towards the issues she cares about and the groups that make a living out of it.

I am curious to know what the aforementioned charitable foundations would actually do in response to funding applications, for example, to improve the educational performance of black Caribbean children that proposes we solve this by tackling teacher racism, given (equally) black African children do well.[95]

Summary

The Sewell report looked at disparate outcomes between ethnic groups and came up with reasons why they persisted, arguing that these were more to do with factors other than racism. For this, its authors were punished severely with much ire poured upon them. The quality of criticism was poor, with standards being of little concern, and facing next to nothing by way of sceptical appraisal. It was almost as if the point was to say something, anything, to create the appearance of discrediting rather than the act of discrediting, for which those involved should be ashamed of themselves.

That is not to say the Sewell report should escape scrutiny, nor does it withstand it in its entirety so long as you know where to look. Its technocratic proposals, on which it flounders, were in fact the sole point on which the critics could find something to agree upon.

The next chapter looks at what the political left has to say on the matter, examining two reports that give us some picture of the report that would have been written were the critics themselves to have appointed the commission responsible for the Sewell report.

2.

Rival takes from the Left

Introduction

There is no end in sight to the number of reviews being pumped out by government and civil society. This is despite the consensus, perhaps the only thing we really all agree on, that everyone has had enough of reviews. This section concerns itself with the critical appraisal of just two, namely the Labour-backed *Lawrence Review* led by Baroness Lawrence and the Runnymede Trust's *Civil Society Report* to the UN Committee on the Elimination of Racial Discrimination (CERD).

The Lawrence Review

That there is something of a review fatigue can be evidenced by a quote from Labour's David Lammy MP, who said,

> 'We do not need another review, or report, or commission to tell us what to do... it is time for action on the countless reviews, reports and commissions on race that have already been completed.'

This quote is sourced from the Lawrence Review, which is another review that tells us what to do.

The Lawrence Review, or *An Avoidable Crisis: The disproportionate impact of Covid-19 on Black, Asian and minority ethnic communities,* to give it its proper title, is authored by Baroness Doreen Lawrence, who is a political campaigner on race, elevated to the House of Lords, and recently appointed as a race relations advisor to the Labour Party. She is also the mother of Stephen Lawrence, who was murdered in 1993 by white racists. The report in question is an official Labour Party publication and thus offers insight into what it is thinking about the priorities of any future government it might lead.

It looks into the effect of the pandemic and lockdown on ethnic minority groups. It finds 'a disproportionate and devastating impact', that minority groups are dying at a 'disproportionate rate' and that they are 'overexposed to the virus', meaning greater economic repercussions. Perhaps unsurprisingly, the government is blamed. The virus has 'thrived on inequalities', such as ethnic minority individuals being more likely to work in healthcare provision or in sectors hardest hit by the lockdown, like hospitality. They are more likely to have 'co-morbidities' which 'increase the risk of serious illness', and face 'barriers to accessing healthcare'. They are subject to 'disgraceful racism' while the virus 'has exposed the devastating impact of structural racism'. It is left for Labour to 'fix the broken system that has left ethnic minority people so exposed'. Lawrence calls for 'systemic solutions to systemic problems'.

Yet despite its insistence on the role of structural racism, this is not defined, and when you try to get close, the review starts to use terms such as 'institutional racism' or 'structural inequality' interchangeably. A definition can only be inferred from the examples given, namely disparate or disproportionate outcomes.

The argument seems to be that we had a structurally racist society, then Covid-19 came along, which meant the structurally racist society had put people in positions where they were more likely to catch the virus, or suffer from the measures imposed to curtail it. Seldom, if at all, does this review distinguish between the virus and government measures to combat it, as though pandemics and lockdowns go hand in hand, when historically, they have not.

The argument for 'overexposure' rests largely on overcrowding and a preponderance for working in occupations that are dependent on personal contact. Ethnic minority individuals are more likely to experience overcrowding, we are told, but not that this is most pronounced in ethnic groups with large Muslim populations, among whom birth rates are higher.[96] They are also more likely to be working in healthcare, or in certain public-facing jobs, and this holds especially for Pakistanis and Bangladeshis in restaurants and driving taxis. That is all true.

But how could this be any different? In what way could we have mass immigration of poor people from poor countries in a way that did not entail clustering within scarce housing, or certain niche sectors? Labour brands this inevitable consequence of its liberal immigration policy as 'structurally racist', when actually the individuals involved have chosen this life. How might these people migrate *evenly* into white-collar office jobs? The most pertinent question must surely be if ethnic minority individuals were any less likely to receive furlough payments or government support, relative to comparable white individuals? That would be the most vital test but it is not undertaken.

Nearly every review on race makes calls for more and better data. Lawrence is no different. Quoted is Dr Chaand Nagpaul of the British Medical Association on Covid-19 data:

> 'Unless we have data we won't know what to do... Data needs to tell us: ethnicity, religion, job occupation [sic], profile of that

> job, whether there was exposure, other medical conditions, info on if they had the right PPE – in order to make sense of this in real time, to understand what is going on.'

This represents too great a faith in the power of data. While the numbers may be revealing, correlation is not necessarily causation. Responses to data should be guided by values and an appraisal of the costs and benefits. Moreover, administrative data are seldom without their issues as to quality and richness.

Lawrence calls for the government to '...mandate comprehensive ethnicity data collection and recording as part of routine NHS and social care data collection'. There is a point, though, where this becomes unwieldy. It represents a boon to advocacy groups as a source of complaints that are hard to disprove, while actually being of little use to clinicians who examine individuals in the surgery or hospital.

The claim made by Lawrence that maternal mortality is five times higher for black women than for white women, and twice as high for Asian women, is one Labour has promoted quite extensively, so it is worth scrutinising. The statistic comes from a report by the campaign group, MBRRACE-UK. While the relative disparity is high, it should be pointed out that the probability, indeed the absolute numbers, are small.

In 2015/17, 209 women died during childbirth, or shortly after giving birth. Of these, at least 29 were black; so around 15 unfortunate women in a single year. That equates to a rate of 38 per 100,000. In percentage terms, that is 0.04 per cent of black new mothers. Of those black women who died, most were black African (22) and most died of 'indirect' consequences of childbirth (22). Ten were born in Nigeria, while seven were of black Caribbean ethnicity.

Moreover, it is inevitable to have an alarmingly high disparity in relative terms, when probabilities are low. While a white probability of 0.007 per cent and a black probability of 0.04 per cent will give you a disparity of over five, the probabilities of not dying will give you a negligible disparity so small as to be not worth reporting.[97]

At the same time, you will not read in the Lawrence Review that ethnic minority people have better health on many indicators. It purports to be in the name of fairness, yet is largely blind to it. For example, it is recommended that the government 'should raise the local housing allowance to the level of local average rents, to ensure low-income households are not forced into debt eviction and homelessness during the crisis'.

Raising housing benefit to the average level of those who earn money to pay rent is not fair on all those who pay their way, as well as eye-wateringly expensive. Moreover, the review calls for a 'rough sleeping strategy' to 'address the causes of homelessness among Black, Asian and minority ethnic communities'. Those white and homeless are not a matter of concern.

There is a paradox at the heart of state multiculturalism, of which the Lawrence Review is an example. It demands more benefits and more regulation but at the same time encourages the idea of 'communities' who are represented by 'community leaders'. For instance, the review says:

> '...for some Muslim communities public health information shared by a faith-based credible source such as the Muslim Council of Britain was more trusted than information received from the Government'.

The problem is Lawrence is accommodating distrust rather than seeking to allay it. On the one hand she wants more governance and on the other, she cannot say you can trust it, for example, if you are a Muslim. Instead, the gap is to be filled by community groups. The example given of the Muslim Council of Britain is curious, in that it is currently cold-shouldered by the government while, according to polling, enjoys the support of two to four per cent of Muslims, with most of that London-based.[98] The Lawrence Review fully vents anxieties over the funding of advocacy groups and demands they have 'effective channels to disseminate information'. All this does is feed the balkanisation of the state, undermining what Labour hopes to expand and occupy.

The recommendations made by Lawrence can be divided into those that pertain to Covid-19 and those to ending structural racism. There is little of any substance. For instance, it calls for 'an urgent plan for tackling the disproportionate impact of Covid', including 'further steps to protect frontline staff and improve public health communication', only no details are offered. A call is made to expedite the Online Harms Bill, while employers must be obliged to publish Covid risk assessment on a central government website.

Ending structural racism is to be achieved through:

- Implementing a race equality strategy – it is said 'we need action not reviews from Government', only the strategy seems largely like a recipe for endless reviews. All departments must 'conduct race audits' and 'produce a roadmap to improve the recruitment, retention, and progression' of ethnic minority people. The Public Sector Equality duty must be enforced, and there should be targets and parliamentary accountability;
- All policies and programmes must help tackle structural inequality – meaning 'racial equality' must be a consideration

in every policy measure. 'Equality impact assessments' to 'shape and inform policy' while the 'socio-economic duty' of Section 1 of the Equality Act should be enforced;

- Mandatory ethnicity pay gap reporting – see Chapter 1 for a discussion;
- End the 'hostile environment' – meaning illegal immigrants should enjoy the same rights as citizens and legal immigrants;
- Reform the school curriculum so that it includes 'black British history, colonialism, and Britain's role in the transatlantic slave trade'; and
- Closing the school attainment gap – the government should 'enforce' a national strategy at 'every stage in a child's development' to ensure equality of outcomes.

The final mistake is to stipulate that the measure for success is ending disparity between groups. As Thomas Sowell must have grown tired of saying, disparity between groups is the norm, always and everywhere. There is no reason to expect groups that are different in all manner of ways to have the same outcomes. This is simply a recipe for race to become the *raison d'etre* of policy making, for an endless supply of bureaucrats to pour over the statistics they scarcely understand, to propose policies as ill-conceived as ethnicity mandatory pay gap reporting, all in the name of the improbable.

Note that Labour's race equality strategy should be 'developed with black, Asian and minority ethnic communities and with the confidence of all those it affects'. The concerns of white people are, once again, irrelevant. In response to this review, Labour has committed itself to a Race Equality Act, details of which we await.

The Runnymede Trust report

The United Kingdom is signatory to the United Nations' International Convention on the Elimination of Racial Discrimination (ICERD). This is an international treaty that commits its signatories to ending racial discrimination and promoting racial harmony. The convention has a complaints mechanism, meaning it has some sort of enforcement capacity. It is monitored by the Committee on the Elimination of Racial Discrimination (CERD).

Every four years, the government, in the guise of the Equality and Human Rights Commission (EHRC), submits a report to CERD detailing the state of the realm regarding its obligations under ICERD. At the same time, a 'shadow report' is written, representing the views of 'civil society' organisations. This is what the Runnymede Trust's report is. It is funded by the EHRC but is Runnymede's take on evidence solicited from a variety of advocacy groups and academics.[99]

The gist of the report is that 'racism is systemic in England and impacts BME groups' enjoyment of rights.' Furthermore, 'legislation, institutional practices and society's customs continue to combine to harm BME groups.' This results in 'disparities' in 'health, housing, the criminal justice system, education, immigration, and political participation'. The situation is worsening, evidenced by disparate risks pertaining to Covid-19 and growing disparity in the criminal justice system.

The equality minister, Liz Truss, is singled out for criticism for a speech in which she outlined the government's commitment to addressing disparity across multiple indicators, particularly geographical. Runnymede takes this as a weakening of its commitment to ICERD and potentially illegal. It further charges that the government is in 'breach of numerous articles' of the convention and makes recommendations that it expresses 'hope' CERD will endorse.

This report purports to be the voice of civil society organisations. Runnymede boasts it has taken evidence from over 100 such organisations, that its report has been endorsed by 78 'NGOs and race equality organisations', and taken 50 written submissions. Looking at the list of participating organisations, it is clear that none of the major think tanks on the centre-right have contributed, nor are dissenting pressure groups such as Don't Divide Us included.

The Runnymede Trust's take can be summarised as 'the government must do something'. A libertarian, such as Thomas Sowell, would say, 'yes there are issues but they are not best addressed by government'. It is thus hard to see how the Runnymede Trust can collate the views of 'civil society' at the expense of using this as a pulpit to spout its own. This is an organisation that has been criticised by EHRC commissioner David Goodhart for descending into 'sectarian irrelevance' while the report in question, he wrote, was 'highly polemical and one-sided'.[100]

Key proof of its partisanship is the report's call for the government to bring fully into force the 'socioeconomic duty', defined in Section 1 of the Equality Act 2010. This is only in force in Scotland and Wales:

> 'An authority to which this section applies must, when making decisions of a strategic nature about how to exercise its functions, have due regard to the desirability of exercising them in a way that is designed to reduce the inequalities of outcome which result from socio-economic disadvantage.'[101]

The rationale for this is that in order to end racial inequality, we must address socioeconomic inequality, since such differences are 'racialised'. It should be pointed out that this is tantamount to what Tony Sewell was saying, in that racial disparity is largely attributable to factors other than race.

Any report that endorses Section 1 cannot be said to be the voice of consensus since the Conservatives argued against this measure while in opposition. The Coalition government further committed to abolishing this, with Theresa May in 2010 damning it as 'socialism in one clause', as 'ridiculous as it was simplistic', and terming it 'Harman's law' after its progenitor, Labour MP Harriet Harman.[102]

On announcing the scrapping of Section 1, May said:

> '... [n]o government should try to ensure equal outcomes for everyone.
>
> 'I want us to move away from the identity politics of the past – where government thought it knew all about you because you ticked a box on a form or fitted into a certain category – and instead start to recognise that we are a nation of 62 million individuals...
>
> 'And despite some of the longest standing and broadest based race equality laws in Europe, some ethnic minorities still suffer inequalities in education, employment and health – estimates suggest that at least 4 in 10 black men could be on the National DNA Database.
>
> 'The answer isn't just more laws, regulations and targets – it's time for a more intelligent approach...
>
> 'Part of the problem with this old approach to equalities was that it categorised millions of people according to what box they ticked on a form. It stopped treating people like individuals and instead viewed them as part of some amorphous herd.
>
> 'The idea that as a person you are defined solely by your gender, by your race or by your religion is as patronising as it is absurd.'[103]

That 'more intelligent approach' later turned out to be the Race Disparity Unit – which aimed to bring about an equality of outcomes between groups, based on data derived from people ticking boxes. It also meant her legacy policy of the 'Office for Tackling Injustices', which aimed to 'look at disparities in areas including socio-economic background' and where they could not be explained, May said, 'I have demanded' they must be closed.[104] This, in principle, is identical to the commitment made in Section 1 of the Equality Act.

The Office for Tackling Injustices exists to this day on paper only. Its creation was endorsed personally by representatives of Stonewall and Operation Black Vote.[105] Section 1 of the Equality Act persists in British law, without being enforced in England. The clear hypocrisy, broken promise, and saying one thing on entering government and another on leaving, leaves a nasty taste in the mouth. As too does the cultivating of organisations who are no natural friends of traditional Tory voters or values.

It should also be pointed out that for all May's talk of 'explain or change', when the evidence was presented to, at the very least, her own special advisor, it was ignored. Alasdair Palmer recalled that in his time as a speech writer at the Home Office in 2013, May's special advisor asked him to write a statement for her on stop and search. He writes:

> 'Part of the motive for doing this, he explained, was political: stop and search is a policy which consistently alienates members of the black community. I was told that it would help the home secretary's standing with Afro-Caribbeans if she made a statement that was critical of the police's use of stop and search. The grounds would essentially be that the tool was racist, or at least used by the police in a racist way…'.

Palmer recounts that he came across a piece of Home Office research from the early 2000s showing that ethnic minority experience of stop and search was often proportionate to the shares of ethnic minority people available to be stopped and searched in the places where the tactic was carried out. In other words, disproportionality was not something to do with race. You would think this would be good news, and yet, according to Palmer, no one in the Home Office seemed to have heard of this study.[106] He continues:

> 'So that is what I put in my draft of her parliamentary statement. The reaction was an explosion of rage from the special adviser, and an emphatic assertion... that statistics on stop and search do not support the idea that it is implemented by the police in a racist way – would not be in the speech. He told me: "Of course I could take this up with the home secretary." But he did not. I doubt she [May] was ever informed that the statistic used to demonstrate police race bias in the application of stop and search was misleading.
>
> 'The special adviser re-wrote the statement in the way he wanted it, with the misleading statistic, and she [May] gave the statement to parliament as he had written it on 2 July 2013. And the rest is history.'[107]

It was to be 'change' regardless of 'explain'. The use of stop and search fell, and subsequently knife crime rose, although the extent to which this is causal is a matter of debate. But clearly in May's own house, the rule was to be overlooking the evidence in favour of the 'racism' narrative. There was actually a better story to be told that might have allayed concerns, allowing the police to build trust. That May's Home Office was determined to reduce stop and search in order to gain political favour, rather than tell the truth, and possibly at the cost of black lives, betrays something rather unsavoury in terms of the regard for black people.

That Runnymede is calling for the implementation of Section 1 of the Equality Act shows its report cannot carry the common ground. This is also repeated in the Labour-endorsed Lawrence Review. As too is its call to end the 'no recourse to public funds' stipulation, while the demands to soften 'hostile environment' policies are also similar. It cannot be the consensus voice of civil society, and the EHRC should look elsewhere or simply save the money. Certainly, it can be questioned whether or not Runnymede and the EHRC have been too close, threatening the independence of both. The EHRC's website has freely promoted publications by the trust, or individuals with an association with it, on its highly partisan 'reading list' on race, since withdrawn.[108] The two organisations have published work together.[109] The Chair of the EHRC, Kishwer Falkner, recently wrote an open letter to Runnymede's director, Halima Begum, in which she said, 'I understand that you meet regularly with colleagues within the executive team at EHRC'.[110] Is this level of access to the state equality regulator offered to everyone?

Reading Runnymede's recent report, it would be fair to say whatever Begum says to EHRC, it is likely to be of little use. It rests on the assumption that statistical disparity between groups is evidence of discrimination, which is not a safe inference when all things are not equal between groups. It is obsessed with the publication of data on *ex post* outcomes, as though they offer evidence of *ex ante* unfairness. Such statistics only guarantee a source of complaints for organisations like the Runnymede Trust, but neither diagnostic nor remedy for whatever problems may lie beneath.

This line of thinking reaches dangerous conclusions in its highly partisan conclusions on the government's anti-extremism Prevent programme. Runnymede writes it is 'extremely concerned' that Muslims are 'still eight times more likely to be referred to Prevent than non-Muslims'. It expresses relief there is 'more balance' in 2018/20 in 'referrals for Islamist extremism and far-right extremism, with referrals for Islamist radicalism decreasing since 2015'.

There is no reason to expect equality of outcomes since there is no evidence to suggest the threats posed are of the same magnitude. Pressuring government to achieve parity will only lead to a reluctance to refer individuals, with potentially catastrophic and bloody consequences.

Runnymede speaks of a rise in hate crime after the EU referendum, without noting the evidence of a sustained decline from the Crime Survey of England and Wales. It further notes a rise in anti-Semitism, but shies away from saying this is largely found among Muslims.[111]

It attributes the greater likelihood of black Caribbean school expulsion to 'institutional racism', without noting that there is no such problem for black African children. It further demands the government discriminate against white people in order to get minority teachers into the profession to make its ethnic diversity match that of the pupils. That is an absurd goal in that Britain's children are more ethnically diverse than its adults due to varying birth rates between ethnic groups. This would lead to poor appointments to the detriment, most of all, of those black Caribbean children Runnymede professes adamantly to care about.

Nor is there any evidence that Runnymede has much faith in civil society. Its recommendations call for greater oversight from the EHRC, more impact assessments, regulation of the media with regard to 'negative or hostile media comment', and regulation of social media. It further seeks to undermine the rights that come with citizenship by removing restrictions on foreigners' access to public services, as well as criticising proposals to reform asylum, echoing Labour proposals.

It further condemns the government's plan to make those who arrive through 'irregular routes' from safe countries – stowaways on lorries or boats crossing the channel – ineligible for asylum. Instead, they urge 'meaningful consultation with refugee and asylum organisations and immigration law practitioners'. What this would mean in practice is the government continue to allow the incentives that encourage people to risk their lives in highly dangerous routes into the country, to continue effectively aiding people smugglers, pushing people into their hands, at great expense to the tax payer and to the misery of truckers in Calais. The organisations Runnymede recommends the government liaise with are simply the vested interests that benefit from the status quo and profess to care. The result would be more arrivals by boat and more lives risked and lost, as well as greater public anger. Again, such a recommendation is both partisan and not representative of civil society opinion on the whole, as well as a luxury belief widely at odds with general public opinion.

Summary

We have now seen what the major players in our debate about race are saying. The orthodox position is that differences between groups are down to race and can be fixed through radical measures, the details of which are not always forthcoming. Sewell's deviation from this stated that differences between groups were largely down to factors other than race.

These two particular reports – Lawrence and Runnymede – do not tell us anything about why disparity exists, nor countenance the truth that it is reasonable to expect. Instead, they fall foul of the logical fallacy of *begging the question*, meaning to assume a point of the proposition in question to be true, and working your conclusions back to this, namely that racism is the primary cause of disparate outcomes. In this light, one shudders at Labour's proposed Race Equality Act – wrong diagnosis and wrong remedy, to which there are consequences.

In the next chapter we look at some of the empirical evidence afresh in order to gauge the extent to which the United Kingdom is a country open to people from ethnic minority groups.

3.

Is Britain really one of the best places in the world for black people?

Introduction

Kemi Badenoch, who is a government minister for equalities, has said that the United Kingdom is 'one of the best countries in the world to be a black person'.[112] This claim was met with the hollow outrage and disbelief that is the currency of our time. But is she right, and on what grounds can we weigh up that claim empirically? And does this extend to other minority groups? Are British Indians better off in Britain than India? Pakistani in Pakistan? Chinese in China, and so on?

The obvious point is that many black people demonstrate their agreement with Badenoch each year through their act of coming to this country as immigrants. There are around 1.3 million sub-Saharan African immigrants living in the United Kingdom, as of 2020, the vast majority black.[113] In 2019, 42,700 people came to live here from sub-Saharan Africa while just 5,800 left.[114] Whatever privations these people may endure, many more black Africans agree with Badenoch than disagree, as revealed by where they choose to live. They would rather be in Britain than in Africa. Moreover, there are people who would sooner risk their lives in crossing the channel in flimsy boats than remain in France or bide their time wating to stow themselves away on lorries at Calais.

The point of this chapter is not to explain disparate outcomes, but rather to gauge the extent to which the United Kingdom is an open or closed country to people of an ethnic minority. This can be done through comparisons across space and time, something which is both more readily done and more fruitful.

Life expectancy

An individual in Britain from any given minority group has a higher life expectancy than an individual living in the country from which that ethnic group originates. A person of black African ethnicity living in Britain has a life expectancy of 82.6 years, compared to someone in Uganda of 60.7, and in Nigeria of just 52.7. That same person has a slightly higher life expectancy than the average white Briton. An individual from the black Caribbean group has the same life expectancy of a white Briton – 81.3 years. Contrast this with an individual in Jamaica who can expect to live 74 years.[115]

This may be down to a 'healthy migrant' effect, meaning that healthier people are more likely to migrate to Britain, and so what you are looking at is a selection effect. It is true that those with better health will be better placed to come. But the disparity between black Africans in Britain and in Africa is too high as to rule out the possibility of a positive effect of living in Britain on longevity. Moreover, why do black Britons compare to white Britons, who are not subject to any comparable form of positive or negative selection?

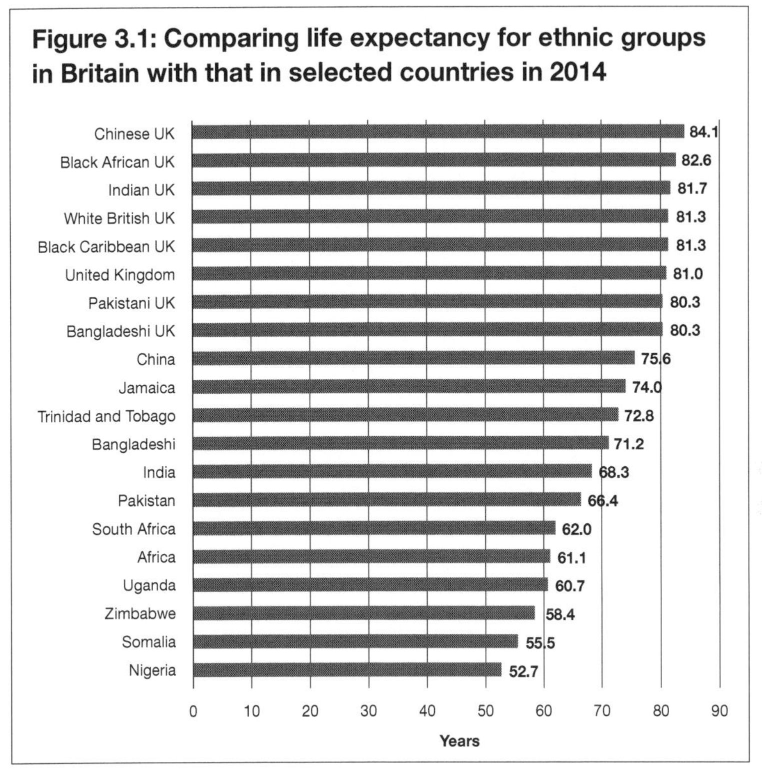

Source: Our World in Data/Integration Hub.

Happiness

While black people live longer in Britain than they do in majority black countries, it is no good if those added years are unhappy and endured rather than properly lived. While it is true that black people tend to be poorer, as do most minority groups, the evidence shows black people to be just as happy as white. When asked to rate their happiness on a 10-point scale, the average score for black people is 7.5, compared to 7.5 for white, 7.7 for Indian, and 7.6 for Pakistani.[116] Happiness is also greater in wealthier countries, and higher in Britain than both South Africa and India.[117] All this would imply that a black Briton, as well as an Asian

Briton, is happier here than he would be in the country from which his family originates.

That there is equality of outcomes in happiness within Britain despite inequality of circumstance would imply that happiness is about making the most of what one has, not some absolute state of contentment. Someone who is poor can be just as happy as one who is rich, providing his work is fair and fulfilling and there are avenues open for advance. Equality of outcomes would imply the existence of the freedom to strive for something better.

Education

Another way to weigh up Badenoch's claim is to look at educational attainment. The Programme for International Student Assessment (PISA) measures the ability of 15-year-olds in reading, mathematics and scientific knowledge. Standardised tests are applied globally to school children that are specifically designed to test ability in a way that minimises any cultural biases in test design. Scores are produced for countries from which rankings are derived.[118]

The following discussion focuses solely on mathematical ability since mathematical concepts are the same the world over, meaning the scope for cultural bias is likely null. In the most recent round of tests, the United Kingdom ranked 18th out of participating countries, with an average score of 502. The top ranked places went to China (591), Singapore (569), Macao (558), Hong Kong (551), Taiwan (531), Japan (527), and Korea (526). Lowest ranked countries were the Dominican Republic (325), Philippines (353), Panama (353), and Kosovo (366). There is a fairly strong correlation between ability and GDP per capita.[119]

Within the United Kingdom, there is variation in mathematical ability by ethnic group. The graph below presents average PISA scores in mathematics across five rounds of PISA from 2006 to 2018. Pakistani, Bangladeshi, black Caribbean and black African students all score significantly worse than the white British. Chinese students do best of all, with an average score in line with majority Chinese-ethnic countries. While this figure is not necessarily statistically significantly different from that of the white British, it should be borne in mind the large confidence interval stemming from small sample sizes.[120]

Figure 3.2: PISA scores in mathematics by ethnicity – average scores 2006-18 with 95% confidence intervals

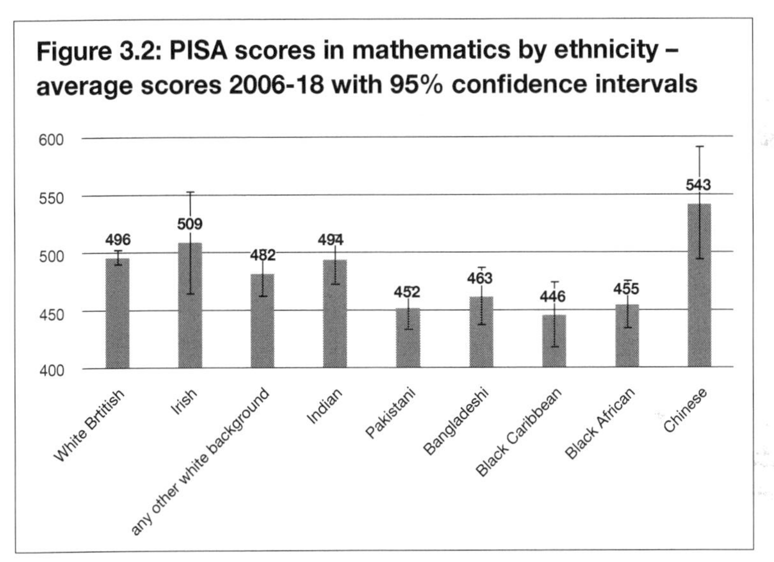

Source: Department for Education.

Participation in PISA is voluntary – with about 80 countries taking place in the latest round.[121] There are no African countries participating, so we cannot compare black African pupils in this country to those in African countries. We do have data on Trinidad and Tobago from 2009 and 2015. In mathematics, that country scored 414 and 417, respectively, less than both black Caribbean children in this country as well as white and black Caribbean mixed race children.

Ethnic Chinese pupils do best both in the United Kingdom and countries where they make up the ethnic majority. Black Caribbean children do worse than white British but appear to do better than in a significant Caribbean country where black Caribbean ethnic children make up the ethnic majority. PISA scores are relatively constant over time, although there is some evidence of black African children catching up in mathematics but not necessarily science or reading, while Indian and white British children hold constant. As too do black Caribbean children.

Figure 3.3: PISA scores in mathematics within the United Kingdom by selected ethnic groups, with 95% confidence intervals

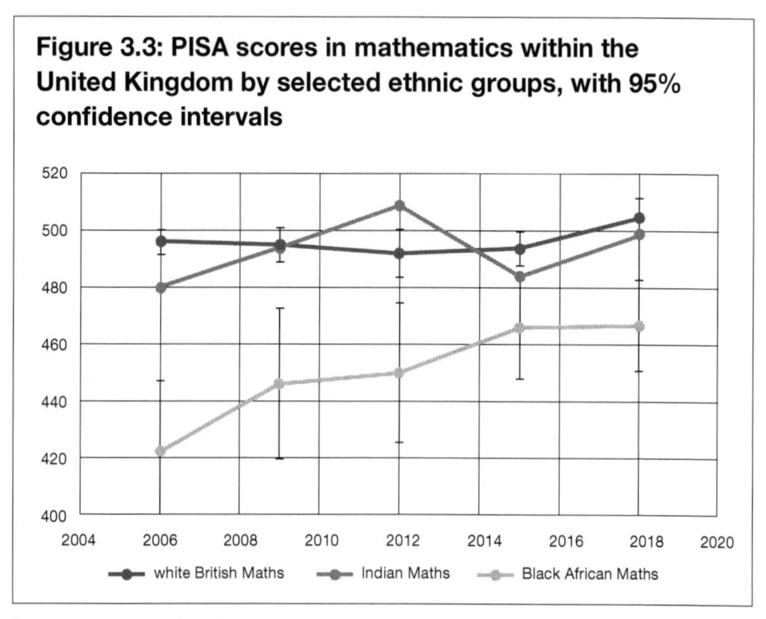

Source: Department for Education.

How is this picture of constancy to be reconciled with GCSE results which show remarkable increases in educational attainment as well as signs of convergence, and both positive and negative disparity between majority and minority ethnic groups? The share of black pupils getting 'good grades' has gone from 23 per cent in 1991 to 59 per cent in 2019 (see endnote for explanation of 'good grades').[122] For Asian pupils it has gone from 33 to 71 per cent over the same period. For white pupils, the corresponding figures are 37 and 64 per cent.

Today, Chinese, Indian and Bangladeshi pupils all outperform the white British. Black African pupils do just as well, while Pakistani and black Caribbean pupils do worse. The worst performance is registered by Irish Traveller and Gypsy/Roma pupils. These differences are not constant, however, as shown in the graph below. While Chinese pupils vastly outperform the white British today, the disparity in getting 'good grades' has grown from an odds ratio of 1.45 to 4.57.

It also used to be the case that there was parity between Indian and white British pupils, as far back as 1991; today the odds ratio is 2.19. Bangladeshi pupils have come from doing substantially worse to doing marginally better, with an odds ratio of 0.28 in 1991 to 1.3 in 2019. This means that in 1991, Bangladeshi pupils did on average 70 per cent worse than white British pupils but 30 per cent better in 2019.

Similarly, black African pupils have caught up with the white British, as have Pakistanis. The black Caribbean group shows a narrowing of the gap between them and the white British between 2004 and 2013, but an increase in subsequent years. This is the only group for whom this is true, although there is a slowdown in the rate of change for most groups in educational attainment in these years. The immediate reforms by the Coalition government in these years included shifting the emphasis back towards summer examinations at GCSE level. Negative disparity is greatest for the Traveller and Gypsy Roma groups, who show no signs of improvement, relative to the white British. Their attainment has gone up since the mid-2000s by about 10 to 20 percentage points.

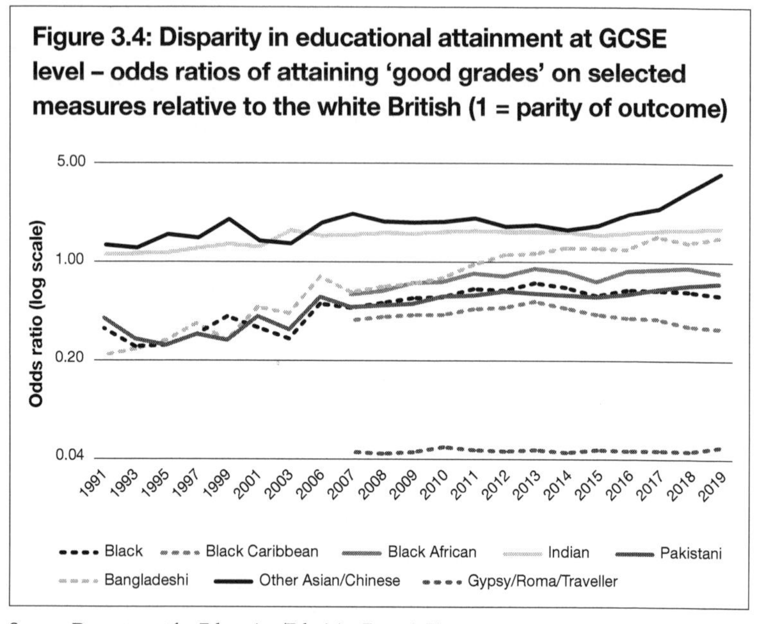

Figure 3.4: Disparity in educational attainment at GCSE level – odds ratios of attaining 'good grades' on selected measures relative to the white British (1 = parity of outcome)

Source: Department for Education/Ethnicity Facts & Figures.

How are we to reconcile the evidence from PISA scores with that from GCSE attainment? The first point is to consider what is being measured. PISA scores purport to measure the ability of a pupil, that is conditional on their education. Pupils are not tested on what they know, but their ability to solve problems using their skills. GCSE results are tests of knowledge based on a curriculum, although they also appraise applied problem solving to some extent too.

That the ethnic Chinese do better than the white British, both at GCSEs and in PISA, and also within both the United Kingdom and in majority-Chinese-ethnic countries, would suggest this has something to do with ability. That British Indians do better than the white British in GCSEs but the same in PISA would imply they simply apply themselves better. The difference in outcomes between black African and black Caribbean pupils is also instructive. That both do worse at PISA than the white British, but black African do as well at GCSE while black Caribbean do worse, and that the amount of racism experienced would be broadly comparable, would suggest this has more to do with variations in effort, performance on the day, and application.

While differences between groups are interesting, the most pertinent fact is the change over time. This shows either that groups are changing in their composition or that the habits of learning can be changed within groups as knowledge of what works is accumulated and transmitted across generations. The fact of groups catching up and overtaking the ethnic majority, or pulling even further away from them, shows that whatever is meant by 'the structure' or 'institutions' and their engrained racism is not sufficient to stymy minority advance in education.

Class

If we look at occupational class, then we see the most prestigious middle-class jobs are more likely to be occupied by white people than black. Using the official NS-SEC 8-fold occupational class classification, we see in 2020 that 12.1 per cent of white British workers are in the 'higher managerial and professional class'. Contrast this with just 7.1 per cent of black Caribbean and 7.1 per cent of black African workers.[123]

A thorn in the eye for those who would say this disparity is down to white racism or 'the structure' is that the proportions for Indian and Chinese workers are about twice as high as those for white British – 24 per cent in each case. Another is that the figure for mixed race white and black Caribbean workers is 10.8 per cent, while for mixed race white and black African workers it is greater, at 17.2 per cent.

Whatever disparity there might be should also be weighed up historically with the insight that ethnic groups have different historical trajectories. One study by Li and Heath provides figures on ethnicity and class, going back to the 1970s for men and women. These data are supplemented by contemporary data from the Labour Force Survey.[124] If we look at the 'salariat', meaning the top two occupational classes of NS-SEC, we see near enough parity between white British and black Caribbean workers, albeit skewed towards Class II in the case of the latter.

There has been a remarkable convergence in chances of access to the salariat. According to Li and Heath's figures, the share of black Caribbean men has grown from 7.6 per cent between 1972/80 to 35.7 per cent in 2020. The corresponding figures for white British men are 21.6 per cent and 35.8 per cent. This convergence is testimony to the accomplishments of black Caribbean men, as well as the openness of British economic life.

Given we recruit our middle-class from the children of middle-class people far more than we do from the working-class, then it is unreasonable to expect our elites to be proportionately composed of the children of nurses and public service workers; occupations in which the initial wave of West Indian workers were largely recruited into. It is reasonable to expect the children of elites in other countries to become elite in this one, as is the case with the children of Gujarati/East African Asians. That West Indians in New York are famed for their *Protestant ethic* of business acumen in the same way, would point towards selection effects in the types of people attracted to specific economic niches within countries.

There is a similar story of catching up for Pakistani and Bangladeshi men, in terms of access to the salariat, while

Indian, Chinese and Irish men have all overtaken the white British. The dip in the 1980s and 1990s pertains to high unemployment, which was more greatly experienced by ethnic minority groups. The exception is the case of black African men, who have fallen behind white British men, with this perhaps reflective of compositional differences within this statistically-defined ethnic group, that is a shift from African elites in the 1970s to greater shares of poor migrants in more recent years.

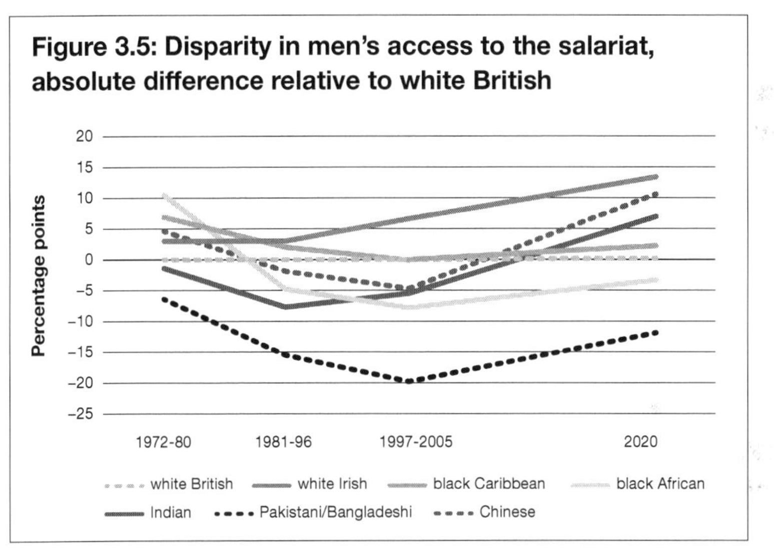

Source: Adapted from Li & Heath 2010/Labour Force Survey.

For women, the story is slightly more complicated. Standing out is the growth of the female Pakistani/Bangladeshi middle-class, from 3.9 per cent in 1972/80 to 18.5 per cent in 2020. Within this predominantly Muslim group, a family model whereby men go out to work while women take care of the home and children, tends to prevail – 34.6 per cent of Muslim women support this model, compared to 13.8 per cent of all women. However, younger cohorts of Muslim women are less in favour, as are British-born Muslim women.

There does seem a strong cultural element influencing Pakistani/Bangladeshi female employment rates. In the United Kingdom it is 30 per cent, comparable to those for women in Pakistan and Bangladesh (22.1 per cent and 29.9 per cent, respectively). Of Muslim women who stay at home, 84.8 per cent had mothers who did not work, while for those women who go out to work, 66.4 per cent had mothers who also worked.[125]

Against this backdrop, the signs are encouraging, only the growth of the Pakistani/Bangladeshi middle-class has not been at the same rate as the white British, meaning an increase in disparity. Indian women have overtaken white British women, while black Caribbean women have always done at least as well, if not better. For black African women, a similar story is evidenced as to men. Chinese and Irish women have surpassed the white British.

Figure 3.6: Share of women in salariat

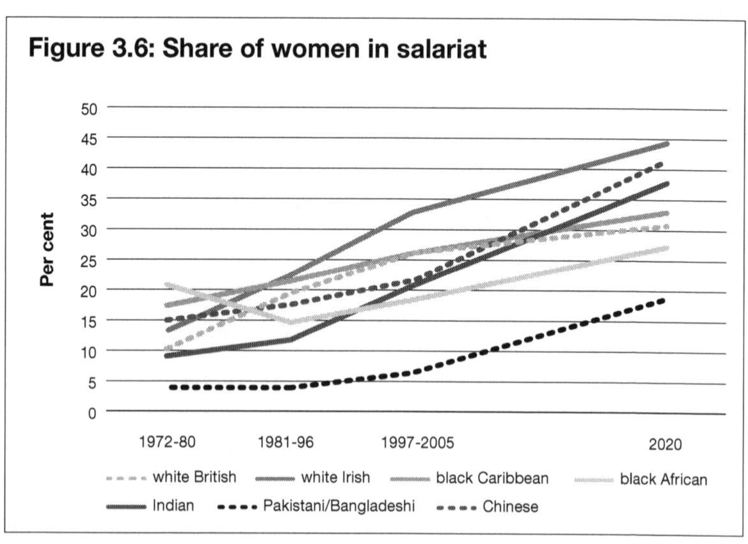

Source: Adapted from Li & Heath 2010/Labour Force Survey.

Britain has undergone substantial changes in occupational classes, with a decline in the share of the working-class, along with high unemployment during the 1980s that particularly impacted on ethnic minority groups. Nevertheless, the evidence is not consistent with one of total blockage to the best-paid and prestigious jobs. Whatever restrictions placed on ethnic minority individuals are, they are not enough to prevent their advance.

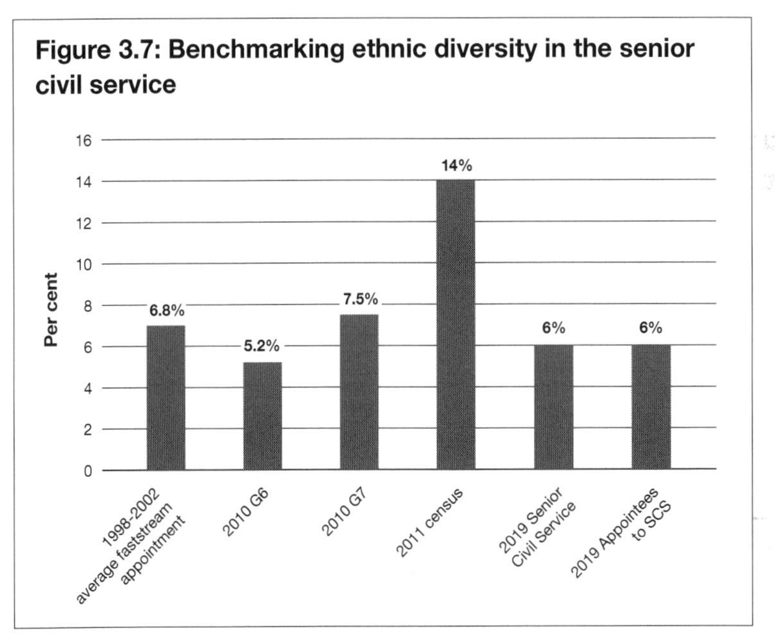

Figure 3.7: Benchmarking ethnic diversity in the senior civil service

Source: Government Statistics/Census England & Wales 2011.

The growth of the minority middle-class can be evidenced through looking at the civil service. This has grown from 9.3 per cent non-white in 2010 to 12.7 per cent in 2019. Over the same period, the senior civil service – the top jobs – has grown from four to six per cent. The discrepancy between the top and the rest is often seen as evidence of either discrimination or a 'lack of representation'. However, this ignores the fact that the senior civil service stands in line with the ethnic diversity of its 'pipeline' positions in years gone by, casting doubt on the extent to which discrimination is pervasive and determines chances.[126]

Something similar can be evidenced in medicine, with the share of consultants having increased from 22 per cent to 36 per cent over 10 years, in line with the shares of junior doctors in the late 1990s and early 2000s, as well as those in intermediate positions roughly a decade ago.[127]

Figure 3.8: Benchmarking diversity among doctors

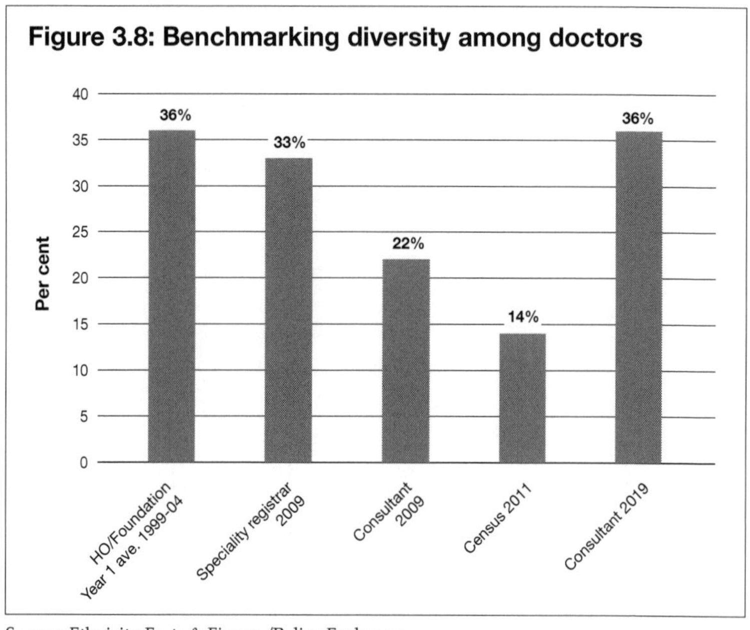

Source: Ethnicity Facts & Figures/Policy Exchange.

Such data prove the futility of using population share as either a benchmark or a target for what ethnic diversity in any given organisation ought to be. Yet, many organisations, including governmental ones, persist in this way, guaranteeing an inappropriate and costly outcome, in terms of decent people put into jobs they are ill-suited for, costing them personally and professionally, while others pay for their shortcomings.

We have seen the extent to which elite jobs are open to black people as well as other ethnic groups. But what about international comparisons? In terms of occupational class, the United Kingdom also has one of the largest black professional classes in Europe, put at 24 per cent by an EU study. Contrast this with France at 18 per cent, Germany at 14 per cent, and Italy at one per cent.[128]

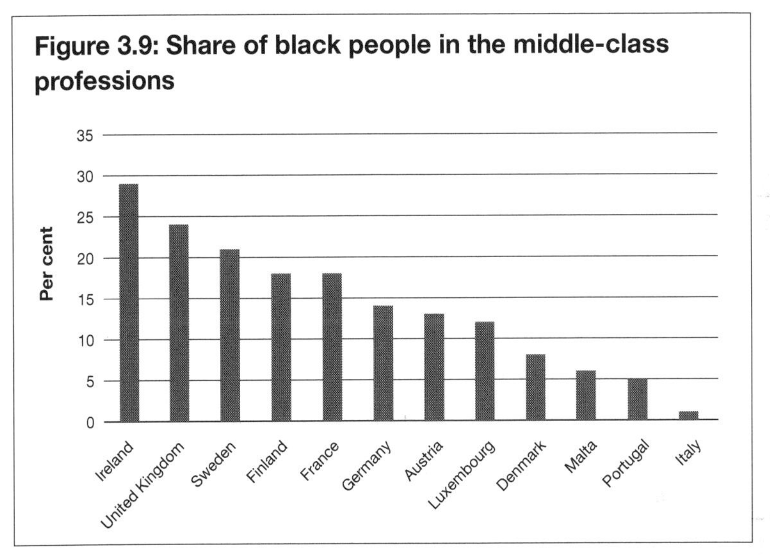

Figure 3.9: Share of black people in the middle-class professions

Source: European Union Agency for Fundamental Rights.

Wealth

It can also be pointed out that wages are higher in this country than in the countries of the Caribbean, Africa, and the Indian subcontinent, and that whatever disparity there is in pay, the average minority Briton will earn more than those in the countries of his familial origin. The table beneath shows differences in individual wealth defined as the value of net financial and non-financial assets, including property. Data are Office for National Statistics (ONS) estimates for ethnic groups within the United Kingdom, set in comparison to the most obvious country of familial origin. Such country data comes from Credit Suisse and may entail differences in methods. A broad comparability is assumed and the results prove insightful.[129]

White British adults have a median wealth greater than all other ethnic minority groups, although Indians are not too far behind. These data do not allow for differences in average age between groups, with older people naturally having more wealth since they have had more time to accumulate it. The median ethnic minority individual in Britain has assets substantially greater than in the country where his family originates from. For example, the median British Pakistani will have 33 times more wealth than the median Pakistani.

To make the test more conservative and to pre-empt any criticism that we are talking about selection effects with more able types having migrated to the United Kingdom, data on low wealth, defined as the 25th percentile within a given ethnic group, are also included in the table below. Individuals at this level still tend to have more wealth than the median person in the comparator country in question. For instance, the black Caribbean individual at the 25th percentile in the United Kingdom has wealth greater than the median Jamaican by a factor of around three. The significant exception to this rule is the Chinese, reflecting China's rapid rise.

It should also be pointed out that disparate outcomes between whites and non-whites are taken as evidence of an assumed truth, namely the existence of a system that benefits white people. Proponents of this argument never bother to explain differences between non-white groups in a manner that is logically consistent, or at all, for that matter. That your typical black Caribbean has more than your typical black African, on such terms, would have to be evidence of how systemic racism favours the former somehow, and presumably *subtly* and *insidiously* as some sort of nefarious tactic of divide and rule. Moreover, what beneficial wealth accumulation there is for minority groups is encouraged, at least for the first generations of immigrants, through transfers of money via the welfare state. One study of the fiscal contributions of immigrants showed that non-European Economic Area (EEA) immigrants take out substantially more than they contribute. In essence, those already here subsidise others to come.[130]

Table 3.1: Individual wealth by ethnic group with country comparators

Ethnicity	Median wealth (2016/18)	25th percentile (2016/18)	Comparator country	Median wealth (2021)
White British	£166,700	£38,000		
White other	£53,200	£11,500	Poland	£17,200
Indian	£144,400	£31,000	India	£2,300
Pakistani	£52,000	£9,300	Pakistan	£1,600
Bangladeshi	£22,800	£2,900	Bangladesh	£2,200
Black Caribbean	£84,000	£13,300	Jamaica	£4,400
Black African	£18,100	£3,900	Nigeria	£1,100
Chinese	£67,300	£3,800	China	£17,600

Source: ONS/Credit Suisse.

Jobs

Unemployment rates are not necessarily lower for people of ethnic minorities here than for their co-ethnics overseas. For example, black people in the United Kingdom have an unemployment rate of eight per cent, as of 2019, compared to 6.5 per cent in sub-Saharan Africa. There are African countries where unemployment is low (for example, Uganda – two per cent) and where it is high (South Africa – 28.5 per cent). Similar trends are observed in the

Caribbean. For example, unemployment is low in Trinidad and Tobago at 3.5 per cent, and moderately high in Jamaica at 7.8 per cent.[131]

It is not necessarily a given that there are more opportunities for employment here, and we know ethnic minorities have higher rates of unemployment on the whole, and endure longer periods out of work. But certainly, the rewards once within work are much higher than for their co-ethnics elsewhere.

Comparing the prospects of black people in the United Kingdom to other European countries also reveals a positive picture. A study conducted by the European Union Agency for Fundamental Rights (EUFRA) published in 2018, showed the country was consistently ranked among the best countries in terms of economic opportunity for black people.[132] As seen in the graph below, the employment rate for black people in the United Kingdom is high compared to other EU countries. The percentage point difference from the general population's rate is also minimal.

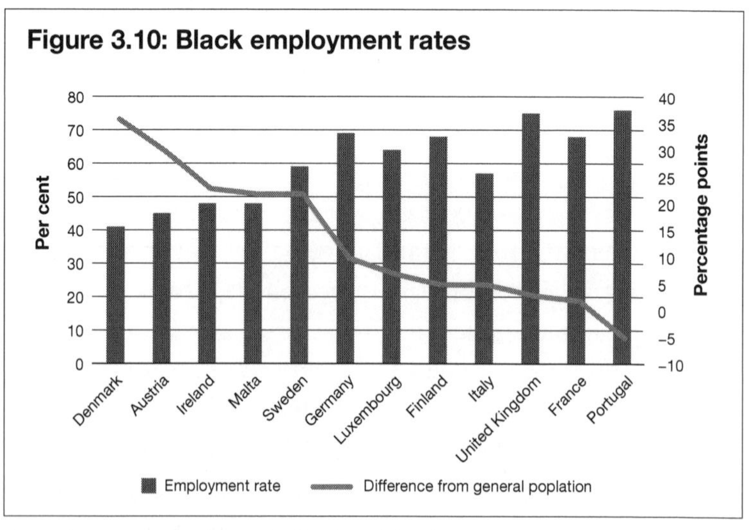

Source: European Union Agency for Fundamental Rights.

The share of those black and aged 16 to 24, and neither in employment nor education – so-called NEETs – is also low in the United Kingdom, at seven per cent. Of those countries studied, the percentage point difference from the general population rate was also lowest, at just under four points.

Figure 3.11: Black people neither in employment nor education

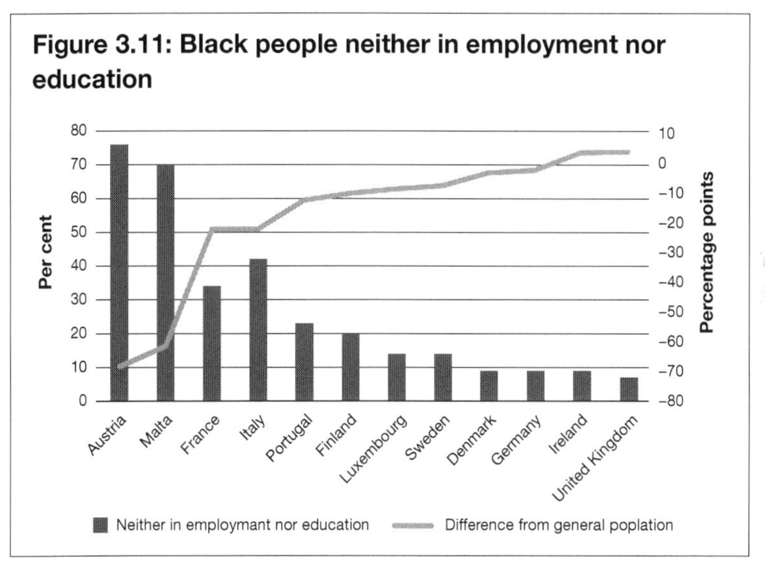

Source: European Union Agency for Fundamental Rights.

This study is perhaps unique in that it allows for some comparison of the fortunes of black people in different European countries. Certainly, the data point towards a far greater degree of economic openness, opportunity and black success in the United Kingdom than in most of the other countries studied.

The costs to living in Britain for ethnic minority individuals

While the good things are appreciated by so many ordinary people, from day to day, they are scarcely acknowledged by those who profess most ardently to care. There are, however, costs that are paid more often by ethnic minority individuals, although they do not have the monopoly on these.

There are three broad types of harm: racial abuse, discrimination, and psychological costs.

Violent and verbal abuse

While abuse based on racial hostility is more likely to be experienced by ethnic minority individuals, it is a rare occurrence. As we shall see, the survey evidence drawn from the most credible academic sampling methods shows the incidence to be both small in any given year, but sufficiently large so that it is likely all ethnic minority individuals will experience it in their lifetimes.

'Hate crimes' are defined as crimes motivated by hostility based on a set of characteristics, including race – 1.1 per cent of black and Asian people will experience a hate crime in given year, compared to 0.2 per cent of white people. Less than one per cent of black and Asian people report being attacked on grounds of their ethnicity. Around seven to nine per cent report experiencing being insulted on grounds of their ethnicity, compared to 0.4 per cent of white British.[133] The evidence further suggests an overall decline in racial hostility experienced by minorities. In 1991, there were an estimated 60 racially motivated hate crimes per 1,000 people targeted against Asians and 82 per 1,000 against blacks. In 2016/19, the corresponding figures were eight per 1,000 and five per 1,000.

In 1993/4, around one per cent of black and Asian people reported being assaulted on grounds of race/ethnicity, compared to roughly 0.5 per cent in 2017/18. Over the same period, 14 per cent of black people experienced a racial slur, falling to 8.5 per cent, while for Asians the corresponding figures were 10.2 per cent and 6.7 per cent.[134]

Such declines are consistent with evidence of declining prejudice, as captured by the British Social Attitudes Survey. In the early 1980s, around 30 per cent of white Britons would object 'a lot' to a close relative marrying a black person, dropping to an estimated seven per cent in recent years. Such sentiments are largely confined to older generations.

People of an ethnic minority are more likely to experience prejudice, but this is likely a matter of numbers since they have their own prejudices too. They are relatively fewer and so are more likely to meet a bigot. Around seven to 10 per cent of black people have strong reservations about a close relative marrying a white person, as do around 10 to 20 per cent of Asians. Around 14.5 per cent of British Indians express strong reservations about a close relative marrying a black person.[135] Polling has further shown between 11 and 15 per cent of British Muslims can be classed as strong anti-Semites, compared to a national average of 3.6 per cent.[136]

If we look at all individuals convicted of racially or religiously aggravated offences, then we see ethnic minority disproportionality. In England and Wales between 2008-18, six per cent of those convicted were black, against a population share of three per cent at the last census.[137]

Victims of 'grooming gangs' often recount being referred to as 'white slags' and worse.[138] Racially-inspired killings are few – no more than five each year. But the most prominent examples of inter-group violence have entailed people from ethnic minorities – radicalised Muslims – killing people indiscriminately.

Making international comparisons is never easy, but the same EU study of black people living in the EU in 2016, when the UK was still a member, allows for this. Surveys found that 21 per cent of black people in Britain reported perceived racist harassment in the five years prior, compared to 32 per cent in France, 41 per cent in Sweden, 48 per cent in Italy and Germany, and 63 per cent in Finland. The same study showed three per cent of black Britons reported perceived racist violence in the last five years, compared to six per cent of black people in France, nine per cent in Germany, and 13 per cent in Austria.

Fourteen per cent of black Britons reported either a family member or friend being called derogatory names, the lowest in the sample, compared to 33 per cent in Germany and 47 per cent in Austria. On most measures, Britain scores well, and usually ranks in Europe among the best places to be black.[139]

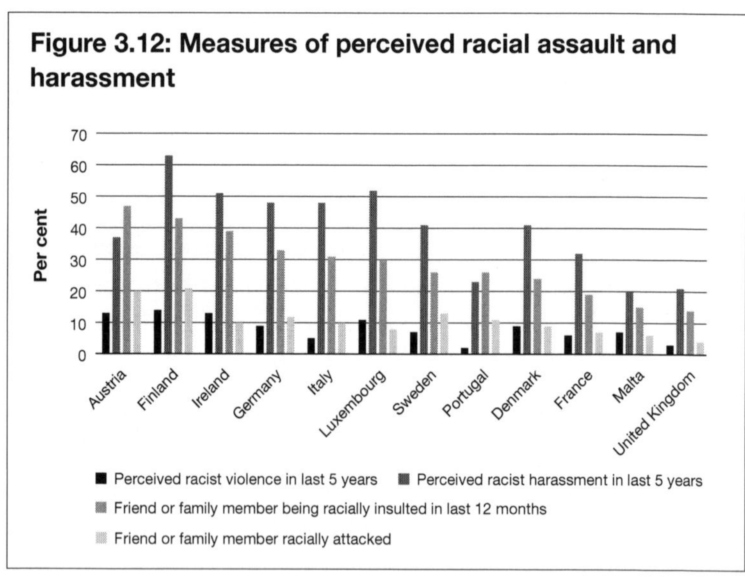

Figure 3.12: Measures of perceived racial assault and harassment

Source: European Union Agency for Fundamental Rights.

Discrimination

The concept of discrimination is tricky to grasp, both conceptually and empirically, because the term has become another of those 'catch-all' concepts that encompass all manner of negative experiences – from being declined a job or opportunity on grounds of race, to being treated differently, to hearing 'discriminatory' language you do not like. We know from 'correspondence studies', or CV-tests, that minorities are more likely to experience discrimination in hiring. We know that they are more likely to perceive it in their hiring decisions, up to a quarter, although the data on the matter are limited in that we seldom find out for sure why we did not get the job. Most, however, regard hiring and promotion decisions as fair.[140]

Such racial preference will likely further manifest itself in decisions over things like rentals and access to schools and nurseries. Recently in Dundee, the politician Humza Yousaf alleged, with some credibility, that a nursery was discriminating against minority children, after his daughter was refused a place while fictitious applications in the names of ethnic Scots were encouraged; allegations rejected by the nursery in question.[141] The EHRC also recently admonished the holiday camp operator Pontins for operating an 'undesirable guest list' of Irish surnames for the purposes of rooting out stays by Gypsies.[142]

The aforementioned EU survey shows that black people in this country report much lower experiences of perceived discrimination than in other European countries. For instance, two per cent of black Britons reported being stopped and searched based on racial profiling, compared to nine per cent in Italy and 31 per cent in Austria.

Three per cent reported discrimination in access to housing, much less than in all other surveyed countries, ranging from around 10 to 40 per cent. At work and in hiring, while the perception is greater for black people in the United Kingdom, it is substantially less than elsewhere

– around 15 per cent compared to at least 20 per cent, rising to almost 50 per cent in countries such as Austria and Italy.

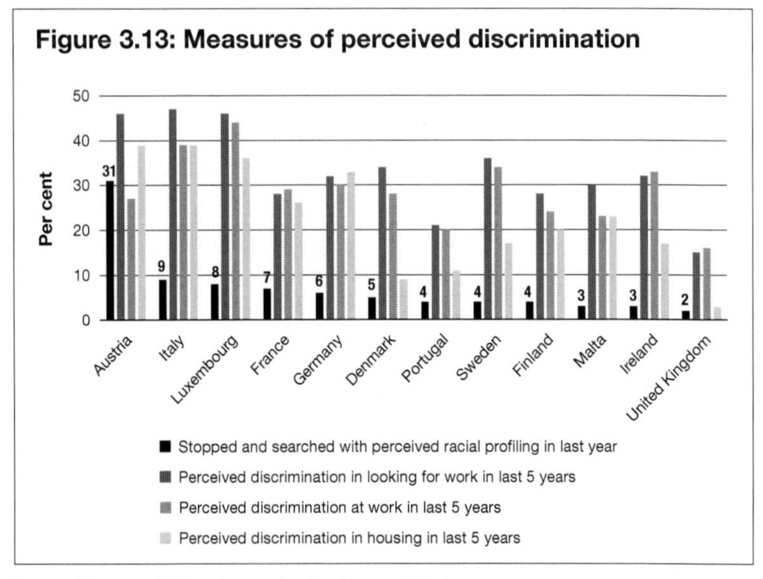

Figure 3.13: Measures of perceived discrimination

Source: European Union Agency for Fundamental Rights.

The issue of stop and search is a tricky one, in that many people are inconvenienced unnecessarily in order to prevent very serious harm to few people. It may also be used as a means of harassment. This is experienced more by black people, with 5.4 stop and searches per 100 black people, compared to 0.6 per 100 white people. Around one in six stop and searches result in arrest, and this rate is roughly comparable for all ethnic groups, something not consistent with a strategy of undue harassment since that would result presumably in a much lower rate for black people.[143]

There is a popular misunderstanding, propagated by the home affairs select committee, that matters are getting worse since the disparity between black and white is rising. In a recent report it noted that the disparity is by a factor of nine, while in 1999 it was five. The problem is that when probabilities are low, disparity is *inevitably high.*

Probabilities of 5.4 per cent and 0.6 per cent will give you a relative factor of nine. If the probabilities were to be 55.4 per cent and 50.06 per cent, then you will have the same absolute difference but a relative disparity of 1.1. If we consider the probability of not being stopped and searched, then probabilities of 94.6 per cent and 99.4 per cent entail an absolute disparity of, again, 4.8 percentage points, but a negligible relative disparity of a factor of 1.05 in favour of whites. Since not being stopped and searched is the other side of the same coin of being stopped and searched, then clearly, relative disparity in this incidence is not a valid measure of fairness since it is susceptible to prevalence.

The home affairs select committee presents an increase in relative disparity from five to nine over the last 22 years, without telling you the prevalence of stop and search has *dropped* substantially. In the late 1990s, the black rate was 14 per 100, compared to today's 5.4 per 100. The absolute difference from whites has fallen from 12 percentage points to 4.8 percentage points.[144]

The question of disproportionality further hinges on the question of *disproportionate to what?* We always compare to a given group's population share on the expectation that they ought to match. There is, simply put, no *a priori* theoretical reason for why they should. None is ever given and seldom asked for. That stop and search rates should be measured up, relative to some measure of *need,* is seldom entertained in official thinking on the matter, for example the shares available on the streets to be stopped and searched or the shares of those involved in violent crime. When this is done, you see stop and search rates are much more proportionate. The home affairs select committee went to considerable and unsuccessful lengths to try and discredit these arguments.[145]

Psychological harm and mental illness

It is this area that things are most difficult to quantify due to the subtlety and subjectivity of the concepts involved. Contrary to the impression that the Sewell report denied this facet of the 'lived experience', it actually contains something suitably nuanced:

> *'There is something, however, in the idea that even in a relatively open society like today's UK a psychological comfort can be derived from looking like the majority of people around you.'*

Complaints are often heard that it is harmful to experience a society where the majority of cultural waypoints refer to white people, and that people of an ethnic minority need to see themselves reflected prominently in order to feel at home. But such potential alienation can be counterbalanced with the familiarity found in ethnic communities, such as the Chinatowns of Birmingham and Soho, Banglatown in Tower Hamlets, or Brixton, or in community and religious centres such as Mosques and Gurdwaras. Religious schools are available to those who want them.

According to figures from the Integration Hub, a project run by David Goodhart in partnership with the think tank Policy Exchange, minority individuals tend to agree there is rarely conflict between their ethnic culture and British customs. The highest levels of agreement are found among Indians (51.2 per cent), black Caribbeans (56.9 per cent), and black Africans (48.6 per cent). Agreement was lower among Pakistanis and Bangladeshis (c.40 per cent). Around 20 to 25 per cent of each group disagreed, with the remainder unsure.[146]

Then there is the issue of so-called 'microaggressions'. This clunky neologism refers to an amalgam of behaviours including the misspelling and mispronunciation of names, insensitive questions, patronising conduct, not being taken seriously, or taken for someone of lesser social standing; for example, lawyers mistaken for defendants or executives for functionaries. These are very real, only they are often just mistakes based on split-second decisions based on limited knowledge. When made, the person responsible will be invariably mortified. From personal experience, people get my surname wrong all the time and I too have been asked, 'where are you *really* from?' due to my rather unusual English/Scottish hybrid accent. Amusing comments have been, 'Wait a minute, do you mean to tell me you're a Brit?', and 'Richard, are you Swedish?', said by a Swede.

Such occurrences are hard to quantify but will be likely fairly common. There is a problem with applying the idea of 'aggression' to what are usually just *faux pas* where no actual hostility was present or intended. They may very well be wearying but the idea of 'death by a thousand cuts' seems hyperbolic.[147]

That this can explain disparity in outcomes is also weak, in that some ethnic minority groups have positive and disparate outcomes. There is also an asymmetry in that only white people are not to be permitted the luxury of being stupid. Nor does there appear to be any fixed definition, meaning the idea can be perilous to critique without unwittingly giving offence.

Trying to prevent 'microaggressions' seems like an invitation to enforce a social environment that is worse than the problem it seeks to allay. One university recently issued guidelines to white students as to how to look at black people, as though that might not make natural and cordial relations between them more difficult. Pandering may induce further the 'snowflake' tendency that sees displeasing but not violent social encounters as unacceptably harmful, tantamount to violence, and necessitating sanctions and censure.

There is a link between being of an ethnic minority and mental illness which is both nuanced and may be linked to the experience of racism. As documented in the Sewell report, there are 306.8 detentions under the Mental Health Act of black people per 100,000, compared with 72.9 white per 100,000. This is set against a higher risk of being diagnosed with schizophrenia, with a relative risk factor for black African people of 5.7 compared to white Britons, 5.2 for black Caribbean, 2.3 for South Asian, and 2.2 for 'white other'.

Sewell cites research to say 'there is a growing and convincing body of evidence that psychosis and depression, substance misuse and anger are more likely in those exposed to racism.'[148] There is also a strong relationship between being an immigrant and developing schizophrenia, suggesting this may have something to do with a sense of dislocation brought on by being on the societal outside. Studies have found that white migrants to majority white countries may also have elevated risks of developing schizophrenia.[149]

Data from *Ethnicity Facts and Figures* shows that 8.3 per cent of black people aged 16 plus had signs of post-traumatic stress disorder, compared to 5.8 per cent of Asian and 4.2 of white British. For black women the figure was 10.9 per cent.[150]

The comfort of belonging

Perhaps the most ineffable quality is the sense of home. To know you belong, to know this is your home; these are the qualities that define a nation. Regardless, we have much data on this. Around 85 per cent of black and Asian people feel they belong to Britain, in line with white people.[151] And around 65 per cent feel they belong to their neighbourhood, again in line with white people.[152]

The greater challenge may lie in convincing people that they belong to each other. It is not a given, that people may arrive in one country from another, to be accepted and treated as kin. Nevertheless, surveys show generally positive relations, with around 85 per cent of black and Asian people feeling people from different backgrounds get on well in their local area, compared to 81 per cent of white people.[153]

Whatever the level of indigenous resistance to mass immigration, certainly the idea of Britain as the property of white people is in fast retreat, with those agreeing that you have to be white in order to be truly British declining from 10 per cent to three per cent over the last 14 years. Since 2009, the share expressing support for inter-ethnic marriage has risen from 75 per cent to 89 per cent.[154]

It is true that there are tensions and a sense that these have been exacerbated by the Black Lives Matter movement. Around one in five Britons say there is a 'great deal' of tension between ethnic groups, while over half believe Black Lives Matter protests increased racial tension, including 44 per cent of ethnic minorities. When a political movement is based upon the idea of one group and its 'allies' pointing the finger at another ethnic group, and damning it as an object of political suspicion, of 'privilege' as they say, then rejection and counter-repudiation are only to be expected.

We lose sight of what genuine community across ethnic groups we have, community being a much-abused word. We take it for granted, as though our record of inter-ethnic relations would not be envied in countries as different as

France and India. We proceed without regard that this peaceful coexistence might be squandered, and it is utterly selfish and reckless to do so.

Structural racism and institutional racism

It is impossible to say how much 'institutional racism' or 'structural racism' any individual experiences, since these have no fixed definition. Sunder Katwala of the think tank British Future has said that evidence from CV-tests is evidence of something 'systemic'.[155] But it is incumbent on him to offer an argument as to how we might pin down discrimination in hiring as a property of 'the system' distinct from the individuals found within.

Moreover, we know where institutions, in the sense of formal organisations, do not exist, patterns of co-ethnic preference do. For instance, Raya Muttarak has shown the 'most common friendship pattern is having co-ethnic close friends', and speaks of a 'pan-ethnic' tendency towards forming friendships with those who are more similar if not entirely the same; for instance, Muslim Pakistanis and Muslim Indians, Japanese and Korean, and so on.[156]

The experiments of Henri Tajfel conducted in the 1970s show how strong the discriminatory or homophilic instinct is. One experiment saw a group of school children randomly (and therefore meaninglessly) assigned as either for the artists Kandinsky or Klee. Thereafter, they showed not only a bias towards those within their group, but also a tendency towards maximising its resources.[157] Again, this discriminatory instinct exists entirely independently of any facet of institutions or structures, since the bias is an artifact of the experimental method. The school in which the experiments took place was not institutionally Kandinskyist or Kleeist, nor could it ever have been.

That is not to say this form of racism *may* not exist, but if anyone says something is institutionally racist, then it is incumbent upon them to (a) provide a robust definition, and (b) some objective evidence for it.

My idea of institutional racism is of rules in any organisation that may be written and specify the favouring of one race over another, sufficient to provide an inappropriate service to any particular individual. This is what was seen in South Africa as well as Nazi Germany. We also saw it in America, and not only under Jim Crow in the South. For instance, Jews were subject to a quota at Harvard lasting until the 1960s and thereby limiting their number.[158] Harvard could therefore be said to have been, in the past, institutionally racist.

Today, it is unlikely to be the case in the United Kingdom that any major company or employer has any such rule. Most have formal declarations of their commitment to equality, while it is enshrined in law for the state sector.

However, there needs to be greater awareness of how diversity and inclusion schemes may spill over into institutional racism. For instance, in the United States, 20.4 per cent of Asian applicants with the highest grades will be accepted into medical school, compared to 58.7 per cent of black applicants with the lowest grades.[159] This is a result of numerous affirmative action policies that seek to favour black students and result in penalizing Asian students, as well as other groups – and this will include Jews. *De jure* affirmative action policies result in *de facto* quotas – and it is fair to describe American universities as institutionally racist today, just not in the way commonly expected.

In the United Kingdom, such affirmative action policies are illegal, although they have their advocates. The home affairs select committee supports ethnic 'targets' for police recruitment with 'remedial measures for failure to achieve these targets'. In other words, quotas, despite admitting these to be illegal.[160] Kalwant Bhopal speaks glowingly of affirmative action in the United States, claiming, 'Research suggests positive benefits for all students when affirmative action is used'.[161] But she fails to account for all evidence to the contrary, including the lawsuits filed by disgruntled Asians.

Our enthusiasm instead lies in outreach programmes that look to increase diversity – so-called 'positive action'. These become *cause célèbres*, such as the campaigns of David Lammy and Stormzy to increase the numbers of black students going to Oxford and Cambridge. What has been missed is that such pressures have resulted in the share of black students admitted being potentially greater than their share of students with top grades, meaning overrepresentation. For example, in 2020, 3.7 per cent of new UK-domiciled students were black, while in 2018, the share of students getting grades AAA+ was 2.2 per cent. (These figures, supplied by Oxford are from different years but still comparable.)[162]

Lammy criticised Oxford in 2017 for practicing 'social apartheid'.[163] At that time, admissions were 1.9 per cent black, in line with the available black talent pool, at 2.2 per cent. Since then, it has risen to 3.7 per cent – nearly doubling. In 2017, the acceptance rate for black African applicants was 12 per cent, rising to 18 per cent. For black Caribbean, the corresponding figures were 13 per cent and 22 per cent. Applications were rising anyway, prior to 2017, from black people.

There is the possibility that political pressure has pushed things too far, where if left alone, they would have resolved themselves adequately. The consequence of this may be people who are bright but not quite at Oxbridge level being mismatched to the level demanded by their courses and unhappy, where they could have been better served and successful elsewhere. In other words, the university offers them an inappropriate service relative to their individual needs, and is thus judged to be institutionally racist.

Such *cause célèbres* may satisfy emotional needs, either in terms of those who indulge in seeing elite universities bashed in the public eye, or those who see attendance as a metric of group pride and prestige. They may also attract the support and attention of politicians such as David Lammy. However, they entail the *imposition* of a third party's expectation on how many students any given university should admit, that is unlikely to match the true number which can only really be found out in the admissions process. The effect of this mismatch is to bring about a form of institutional racism.

It should also be pointed out that if there is 'underrepresentation' at Oxford, it is for Pakistani and Bangladeshi students. They make up two per cent of admissions in 2020, the rate of change is far slower than that of black admissions, and compared with 3.7 per cent of students getting grades AAA+. Acceptance rates are at 10 per cent.[164] This group lacks the same level of political organisation and popular advocacy, and so few people care.

The discussion has focused on institutional racism, which can be a real concept so long as it is defined as a property of institutions, not the individuals found within them. Concerning structural racism, this is largely defined as inequality of outcomes by those who stress this as both factual and causal (see Chapter 6 for an example), yet that is an error in that it is impossible to show how this is not simply the natural state of affairs between groups that are different in so many ways.

Violent death

While minority Britons can expect to live longer than those in their countries of familial origin, as well as for some groups, marginally longer than the white British ethnic majority, their lives are more likely to be ended abruptly and violently. This is, however, something mercifully experienced by very few individuals. Each year, around 600 people are murdered here in the United Kingdom, the majority of them male. Black people are most likely to be murdered, although the absolute numbers are small.

According to research by Cambridge academics led by Sumit Kumar, there were 5.2 murders of black people per 100,000 population, compared to figures of 1.4 per 100,000 and one per 100,000 for Asian and white, respectively. We are talking about no more than 100 unfortunate black individuals each year.[165]

The rate for black people is down on that for the 2000s when it was around seven to eight per 100,000. However, it has been creeping upwards in recent years, and the trend follows the economy, with it falling as the economy went into recession at the time of the financial crisis – to a low of 2.9 per 100,000 in 2013/14. Rates are more pronounced for young victims. Kumar et al.'s research shows that the black homicide rate for black youths (aged 16-24) is 16.5 per 100,000, compared to 0.7 per 100,000 for white youths. What is staggering is that around half of black murder victims are young. The white youth murder rate is *marginally* less than that for all whites, while the black youth murder rate is 10 points *greater than that overall.*

In my time living in Peckham in London, there were two fatal stabbings in my neighbourhood. The first was a young man who was stabbed to death after an argument. As bystanders gathered afterwards, I overheard an elderly black woman say, 'it's black people killing black people for no reason', and she was right. Statistics show that 80 per cent of black victims had a black principal suspect (in cases where ethnicity is known and a suspect identified).[166] The second murder took place in East Dulwich and involved a black man stabbing to death another over an argument about cigarettes.[167]

Murders involving knives and firearms disproportionately involve black people, with 23 per cent of victims killed using knives being black, as are 39 per cent killed with firearms, compared to three per cent of the population at the 2011 census. Sixty-five per cent of black homicide victims are stabbed to death. The evidence would also point towards a greater likelihood of black people being murdered by strangers over arguments. Where a suspect is identified, around half of black homicide victims are killed by a stranger (43 per cent) compared to 30 per cent of white victims. Forty-one per cent of black victims are killed in the street compared to 17 per cent of white. And where the assailant is unknown to the victim, at least 60 per cent of black victims are classified as killed over a 'quarrel, revenge or loss of temper'.[168] Indeed, the East Dulwich murder involved the murderer telling the court that his victim telling him to go and buy his own cigarettes 'got his defences up' and so he pulled a knife.[169]

Sociologists have written of 'honour cultures' – where perceived insults or affronts to status are punished severely. While honour cultures have existed among whites in the American South, as well as all over the world, it is possible that we have a similar dynamic among black male youths here in this country. While it might be argued that this stems from a frustration whereby black males are denied status by a racist society, such explanation flounders in that

Asians have nothing like the murder rate of black people. Such reasoning only serves to reduce the responsibility for what is always a heinous crime, and for which there are no excuses.

An anonymous junior doctor recently wrote an article for *Unherd* about how London hospitals are witnessing gang-related knife attacks within their premises. Although not stated, both perpetrators and victims will likely be black. Basically, someone is stabbed and then the attackers guess which hospital they are taken to, and come to finish them off. The article makes reference to a practice known as 'bagging' – whereby someone is stabbed in the rectum, necessitating them to use a colostomy bag for life, and intended as the most severe form of humiliation.[170]

While this all makes for fairly grim reading, it is worth pointing out that the British murder rate is low, globally. Britain ranks 149 in the world, with a murder rate of 1.3 per 100,000. Contrast this with a rate of 47.4 per 100,000 in Jamaica, 36.1 per 100,00 in South Africa, or 34.5 in Nigeria.[171] Note that these are substantially higher than the black British murder rate of 5.6. Moreover, Asian murder rates in Britain are somewhat less, to varying degrees, than in Asian countries.

This would point towards variance in the value placed on human life across the globe that is mirrored within the United Kingdom, only to a lesser degree. Again, this points towards Britain being a better place to be black or Asian, regardless of what problems there might be.

While there is a pattern whereby majority black countries tend to have substantially higher murder rates, this is not to do with race but more likely, societal disarray. High murder rates are found in places like Mexico and Colombia (drug-related) and Venezuela (economic collapse). Also, African countries such as Senegal, Burkina Faso and Ghana have murder rates almost as high as the United Kingdom's. There is thus no determinacy pertaining to race. Pointedly, those who make great show of saying 'black lives matter' seldom wish to talk about young black people losing their lives in this terrible and brutal, tragic manner. Their lives are as important as anyone else's.

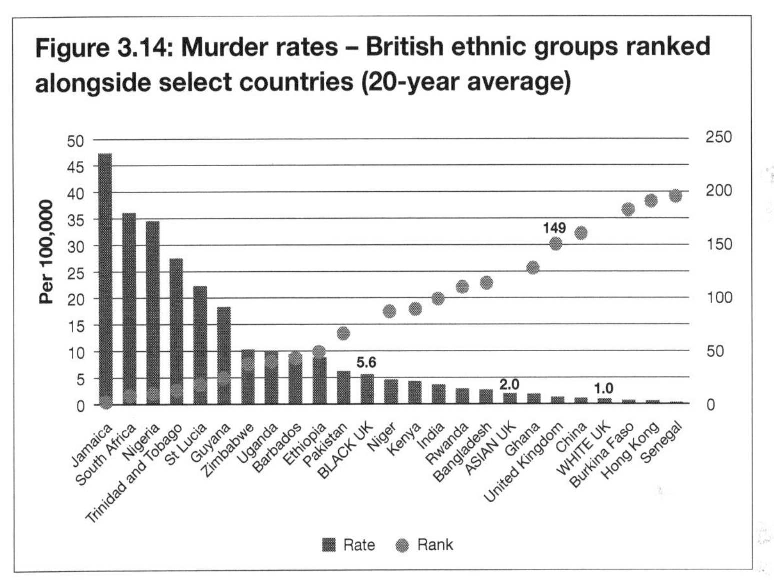

Figure 3.14: Murder rates – British ethnic groups ranked alongside select countries (20-year average)

Source: World Bank/Kumar et al. 2020.

Summary

I have tried to give an empirical account of the extent of some of the harms experienced by people of an ethnic minority. The evidence shows these to be real and experienced by most over a lifetime, but far from typical in a given year. I showed that Britain scored well in terms of low levels of racial abuse, discrimination and harassment meted out to black people.

The study referenced was based on subjective appraisals,

and so to say otherwise is to deny the 'lived experience' of a representative sample of black people living in Britain as well as other European countries. It is 'gaslighting' most foul. The swathes of people gathering in Calais or arriving on our shores is no accident. They know life is better here. Further missing is an appreciation that such costs are near inevitable, in that human beings have a 'groupish' instinct and restrict the extent to which they are willing to share within their 'in-group' at the expense of outsiders. At the same time, racism has declined and the British have redefined themselves to include those who trace their origins elsewhere.

Largely, the costs are those associated with not belonging. In some instances, they can be extreme. Britain's minority ethnic groups are here because of immigration. They are either immigrants or their descendants, as a result of a choice made to come here. The benefits of belonging could have been felt elsewhere but then, the economic benefits of living in Britain could not. There is an inevitable trade-off.

While things are not fair, the benefits to living in Britain are almost entirely absent from our national conversation, which is dominated by undergraduate-level narratives of oppression. The benefits are far greater, and can be summarised as better health, greater safety, better education and more wealth. Moreover, Britain offers a better deal than all its natural European comparators, yet all we do is damn the 'system' that makes this possible. The proposals for its replacement have yet to materialise. The costs are declining and the country has reimagined itself noticeably so that race is not definitive of national belonging.

Finally, comparing between countries and within this country across time reveals a picture of openness far greater than whatever closure there undoubtedly is.

4.

The 'left behind' white working-class

Introduction

This chapter looks at the recent political discourse on the white working-class, as characterised as 'left behind' and needing some sort of help from government. This is treated as a variant of identity politics, not its antidote. It is argued that this subset is not enduring any especial hardship, despite significant problems within it. It is further argued that working-class people have been penalised by past government education reforms to try and help them.

It is shown how 'graduatisation' has increased the costs of 'making good', of reaching the middle-class while the apprenticeship levy has caused the supply of apprenticeships to shrink up. Proposals to improve the poor performance of working-class white people, or anyone else for that matter, will not bear fruit unless they tackle the mindset that is so commonly associated with such circumstances.

Can the government favour the white working-class?

Recently, the education select committee, chaired by Conservative MP Robert Halfon, published a report called 'The forgotten: How white working-class pupils have been let down, and how to change it'. It argues that the 'white working-class' is a 'left behind group' that has endured 'decades-long neglect' and has been 'let down'. This is manifested in this group having the worst levels of educational attainment. In order to correct this, government action is needed, specifically to target the white working-class using better data along with more support.

Better data includes the recommendation that the government draw on the approach of the Social Metrics Commission 'to develop a metric of poverty that provides a better understanding of the nature of poverty by drawing on lived experience'. Support includes the provision of 'family hubs', which are not well defined but seem to be the state's way to provide the knowhow as to how to raise a family.

This report looks to target children who are struggling in school, based on race. While not quite explicit, it calls for tweaks to school funding, including the 'pupil premium' to 'target funding to address attainment gaps, such as that which persistently affects disadvantaged white pupils'. Elsewhere, the report is more explicit, and it is clear that poor white children are to be favoured.

However, there are two key facts that are overlooked. Firstly, that poor black Caribbean children do just as badly.[172] Reading the select committee's report, it is easy to imagine that those poor and not white would be asking, 'what about me?' We should not prioritise any race or ethnic group, but rather concern ourselves with individuals where there is need.

Secondly, working-class whites are more likely to avoid unemployment than those not white and either middle- or working-class in origin.[173] While the returns to schooling are less, it does not result in worse outcomes in the labour market at group level. Perhaps the most significant omission is that we are not told what extra funding for schools actually buys. Nor is the Social Metrics Commission's track record in designing 'metrics of poverty' something that escapes criticism.[174] Moreover, from my own personal 'lived experience', poor performance in a majority white working-class school was largely attitudinal, with pupils competing to get the most unremarkable grades and academic effort punished through derision. This will not show up easily in statistical studies.

Identity politics standing on its head

As I have previously argued, those who advocate for the white working-class are 'intersectionalists' and are promoting identity politics; they do not reject it but rather say we are looking at the wrong victim group. The usual concomitant of identity politics is political clientelism, whereby politicians look to divert money to 'identity blocks' via self-appointed community leaders who will then seek to deliver block votes.[175] The Runnymede Trust has made the argument that the Tories are looking to funnel money to disaffected whites in order to retain its newly found stronghold in the so-called former 'red wall' seats of the North of England. If true, then the problem is that it becomes too expensive not to vote for the party handing out the goodies, and so the democratic choice of free Britons becomes restricted.

Let us hope this cynicism is not underlying the education select committee's report, which was rejected by Labour, although it should be pointed out that those who shouted the loudest are often the ones to argue for special treatment based on race, only for those who are not white.

Who is left behind, really?

Politicians, charities and civil servants like to talk about those who are 'left behind'. It is one of those many terms that is appealing but tends to mask more than it reveals. This imprecision suits them as they can find ample room to present themselves as providers of 'solutions'. But who precisely is 'left behind'? Who has 'been taken with'? And who is this fickle *great companion* who takes along some but not all?

We speak of 'left-behind' areas as though there is a responsibility of those in affluent areas to provide for them. The expectation is that money be taken from those who are successful in life and given to those who are not. But the only way that people have been left behind is by other people who have done something in order to be successful.

According to Daniel Laurison and Sam Friedman, 38.7 per cent of people born to working-class families do not go on to join the professional classes. In some sense, they may be described as 'left behind'.[176] Another way to conceive of the 'left behind' is to consider geographical movement, namely to look at the shares of people who stay close to where they were born. While not a perfect measure, this can be assessed by looking at the shares of people who live close to where their mothers live. Data from Understanding Society show that of those born here, are white British and from a working-class background, 45.4 per cent live within 15 minutes of their mothers, and a further 20.7 per cent within 15 to 30 minutes.

This compares to a national average of 37.1 per cent living within 15 minutes and 17.1 per cent within 15 to 30 minutes. What this implies is a greater rootedness among the white working-class, although familial proximity is the norm for most people. These figures suggest substantial numbers are 'left behind', implying the term itself has no meaningful application empirically.

Nor is living close to mum a bad thing, depending on the mum. Such statistics do have some sort of connotation with failure, however. But asking those who are white British, of working-class origin and living within 15 minutes of mum, to rate their financial circumstances, just 7.3 per cent reported some level of difficulty, in line with the national average.[177]

This implies that the vast majority of the white British working-class are doing fine. They are not victims, nor a poor 'problem class' necessitating saviours any more than any other ethnic group. Of those that do struggle, the reasons for this may be attributed to misfortune of birth, wider environmental misfortunes, or matters of the heart.

Any interventions to help these people must be planned in full knowledge of the fact that the majority of this particular demographic, the white working-class, is getting on perfectly well, or at least perceives itself to be so. Government help may not help, in that it merely saps the work ethic while rewarding fecklessness, and in addition may undermine those who have worked hard, for whom excessive benefits are seen as insulting.

People do not happen to be middle-class, as though it were an accident of birth or something assigned randomly. Instead, they or their parents, grandparents or ancestors have done something that has elevated them from a condition of poverty into the middle-class and sustained them there. This may be passed on from generation to generation, but family wealth has to be nurtured not squandered, and this entails effort. Attempts to 'redistribute' wealth that do not take into consideration the facts of purposeful economic behaviour on the behalf of those successful, risk undermining the efforts made, while being, up to a point, unfair.

Apprenticeships

The education select committee calls for tweaks to the apprenticeship levy in order to benefit white working-class youngsters. The levy is a tax on employers that is set aside for funding apprenticeships – with the aim being to create more. This has been a policy disaster for the working-class, introduced by the Tories.

Prior to its introduction, the number of people undertaking apprenticeships had risen to a high of 908,700, up from 806,500 in 2012. Since the introduction of the levy in 2017, they have fallen to 719,000. Moreover, the decline has been in the sorts of apprenticeships that lead into a career in skilled manual labour, as seen in the graph below.[178] What the levy has served to do is to cause the sources of funds for apprenticeships within employers to dry up, rather than to supplement them. The explanation would be that it became harder to justify funding within company budgets when it could be sought elsewhere. Its administration has also been criticised as overly bureaucratic.[179]

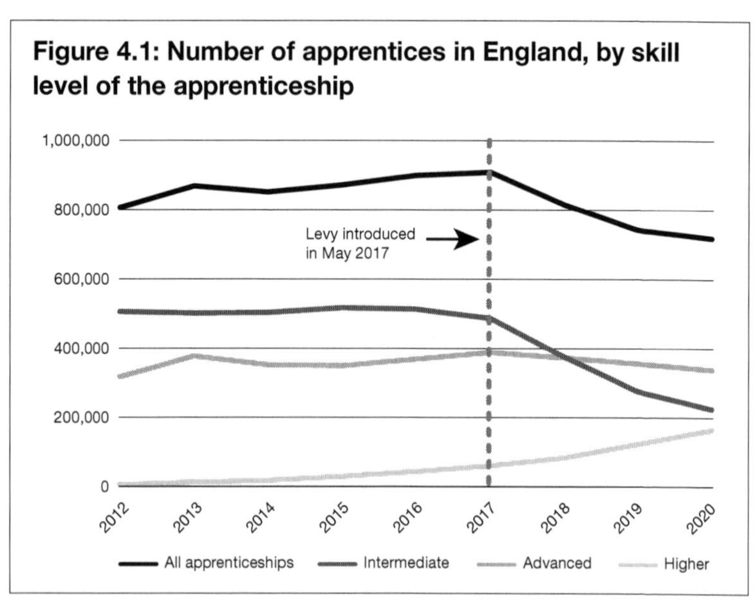

Source: Department for Education.

Furthermore, it is white and black people, presumably working-class, that the levy has punished the most. Data on apprenticeship 'starts' by ethnicity show that while the Asian and 'mixed' groups have more or less held steady since 2011/12, in the cases of black and white groups, the numbers have fallen quite sharply. Between 2011/12 and 2018/19, the number of new apprentices who were black fell by 22 per cent, while for those who were white, it fell 27 per cent.[180]

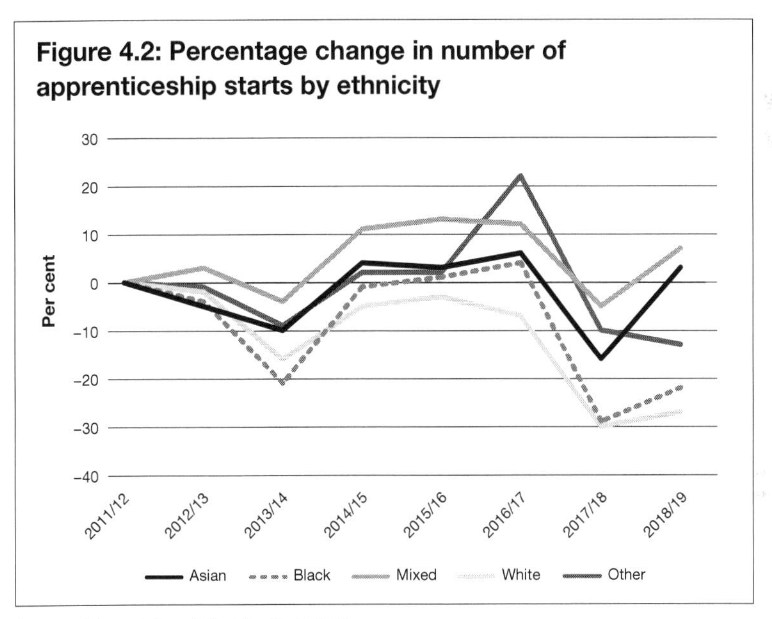

Figure 4.2: Percentage change in number of apprenticeship starts by ethnicity

Source: Adapted from Ethnicity Facts & Figures.

If you have introduced a policy to make things better that has made things worse, it would seem scrapping would be more appropriate than tinkering. But the government will be reluctant to admit its mistake as well as give up on the levy since a small fraction of it now exists to administer it. There is also no guarantee that the damage is not lasting and that in event of its repeal, things would go back to how they were, although the incentives would point in that direction.

We don't need no higher edu-kay-shun

The education select committee calls for universities to spend more recruiting white working-class kids, as an 'underrepresented group'. This though may not be the right approach in that higher education is not the right way for non-academically minded children, and there is a social gradient in cognitive ability, since greater levels are required for professions such as medicine or accountancy.[181] Moreover, the university sector seems already bloated and resentful over our leaving of the European Union.

As David Goodhart has documented in his book *Head, Hand, Heart,* we are seeing declines to the 'graduate premium' in pay, as well as increased disquiet among graduates working in jobs that do not require a degree.[182] Moreover, this is all funded by student loans, of which it was estimated in 2014 that 45 per cent would go unpaid, meaning they are met by the tax payer.[183] In Scotland, higher education is fully funded, directly through taxation. The successful pay to educate themselves as well as those for whom the education bears no fruit in the labour market.

Many of these degrees are largely unnecessary. As seen in the table below, in 1991, those whites who were working-class in origin but working in the higher professions got there on a graduate share of 28 per cent. In 2018/19, that share was 59 per cent. In 1991, if you were white, you could reach the higher professions from the working-class with just GCSEs – 20 per cent of this subset. In 2018/19, that figure was nine per cent. Of those white and born into the working-class and who have stayed working-class, in 1991, only one per cent had a degree, compared to 11 per cent in 2018/19.

Table 4.1: Highest qualification of those in combined occupational classes, by ethnic and class origin

Present occupational class	Ethnicity/ class origin	Year	Unweighted N =	Degree	Other higher education	A-level	GCSE	Other qualification	None
Classes 1 & 2	white middle	1991	231	56%	9%	20%	10%	4%	1%
Large employers & higher management		2018/19	659	80%	9%	7%	4%	1%	0%
Higher professional	white working	1991	252	28%	14%	27%	21%	4%	6%
		2018/19	431	59%	13%	15%	9%	4%	1%
	minority middle	1991	15	80%	7%	7%	7%	0%	0%
		2018/19	66	92%	5%	2%	0%	2%	0%
	minority working	1991	20	40%	25%	35%	0%	0%	0%
		2018/19	40	75%	8%	13%	3%	3%	0%
Present occupational class	**Ethnicity/ class origin**	**Year**	**Unweighted N =**	**Degree**	**Other higher education**	**A-level**	**GCSE**	**Other qualification**	**None**
Classes 3 & 4	white middle	1991	771	23%	18%	22%	27%	7%	4%
Lower management & professional		2018/19	1616	58%	15%	17%	8%	2%	0%
Intermediate	white working	1991	1234	8%	13%	20%	34%	13%	12%
		2018/19	1682	36%	20%	22%	18%	3%	2%
	minority middle	1991	20	30%	25%	5%	15%	20%	5%
		2018/19	157	70%	13%	10%	5%	1%	1%
	minority working	1991	35	31%	17%	14%	31%	6%	0%
		2018/19	141	58%	16%	18%	6%	2%	1%
Present occupational class	**Ethnicity/ class origin**	**Year**	**Unweighted N =**	**Degree**	**Other higher education**	**A-level**	**GCSE**	**Other qualification**	**None**
Classes 5,6,7 & 8	white middle	1991	549	5%	6%	24%	36%	12%	17%
Small employers & own account		2018/19	956	29%	14%	23%	24%	8%	2%
Lower supervisory & technical	white working	1991	2034	1%	2%	17%	28%	13%	39%
Semi-routine		2018/19	1939	11%	10%	26%	32%	13%	7%
Routine	minority middle	1991	19	5%	0%	47%	16%	21%	11%
		2018/19	71	41%	11%	18%	16%	7%	7%
	minority working	1991	75	4%	4%	13%	17%	21%	40%
		2018/19	171	19%	16%	22%	22%	11%	11%

Graduatisation has increased the dominance of the universities, of middle-class Brexit-loathing academics as the gatekeepers into middle-class affluence. All this can be traced back to Tony Blair's figure pulled out of thin air of 50 per cent of young people going to university. There is a right number of university graduates and infinite wrong ones, but not one that can be known by politicians or civil servants. Too high a figure means waste and opportunity costs in that we do not learn the skills we need, on which a career that offers satisfaction and prestige can be built. If working-class individuals of any race wish to get on, today they have to do far more than their parents ever did, paying more money and incurring huge debts to people who despise the politics based on patriotism that working-class people are most likely to endorse.

Summary

There are no victim groups in British society, but rather individuals who can be aggregated into groups by statisticians and then adjudged to be better or worse performing. The reality is you have some individuals who do well and others who do not. Efforts to help them will only work if they tackle what is not so readily available to statisticians, namely positive educational and work ethics. Blunt measures, imposed from on high, such as a target for the numbers going to university or an apprenticeship levy, have unintended consequences that will often penalise those they are intended to help.

5.

What happened at the Euros?

Introduction

This chapter takes, as a case study, the fallout from the European Championships in football which took place in the summer of last year (2021). It is presented as an acute example of how our conversation on race has the power to divide and to sour moments which ought to be savoured.

England manager Gareth Southgate has created the most successful England football team since Sir Alf Ramsey. He has led England to a World Cup semi-final and a final of the European Championships, where they lost on penalties. He has re-established the English national team as a major force in international football and restored national pride, all accomplished with a group of players who play for each other, despite club rivalries, but who do not have quite the ability of the *golden generation* of Beckham *et al*. This has not necessarily been welcomed by the Scottish. Yet the level of acrimony at the end of the European Championships of June this year was far greater than even after the dire showings of past teams led by Roy Hodgson and Kevin Keegan. How on earth is this possible, when the English nation should have been feeling good about itself?

There are two issues that are related. The first is the racial abuse aimed at the three black English players who missed penalties in the final – Rashford, Sancho and Saka.

The second is the 'taking of the knee' ritual conducted by the English players before each game, which persists in the Premier League as well as in some other sports. The two are linked.

Online abuse of black players

It is difficult to gauge how many abusive messages were sent via social media websites, either directly to the players or making mention of them, nor their exact nature. Pundit and former England player Rio Ferdinand described how, '[i]mmediately after the game social media platforms became the toxic and racist safe place for the ignorant and cowardly rats to start spouting their disgusting feelings'. But *The Sun* reported just 1,000 posts were deleted by Twitter.[184] To put this in perspective, there are at least 350,000 'tweets' sent per minute.[185]

Then in August, we learned the police received 600 reports of racist comments sent to black English players, with 207 adjudged to be criminal. Of these, 123 came from abroad while just 34 were domestic. As of 5 August 2021, 11 people had been arrested, and face penalties of up to two years in jail. Bringing these people to justice, according to Chief Constable Mark Roberts, who is the National Police Chiefs Council lead on football, had entailed a 'vast amount of work'.[186]

Screenshots of the abuse published by the *MailOnline* show 'emojis' of monkeys sent by accounts with names like 'rss777.7', 'mad_england', and 'elenaxoxo8'.[187] Other accounts, such as 'alexnavarette36', used racial expletives. The same screenshots reveal messages of love and support for the players, and the message from the great and good has been universally one of condemnation. Four people have been arrested, including one man who wrote: 'Marcus Rashford that MBE needs burning ya fake. Pack them bags and get to ya own country.' The man responsible initially claimed his phone had been hacked, and then that he had been drunk at the time of posting.[188] It was further found that 105 Instagram accounts had posted racial abuse, with just five UK-based.[189]

Many abusive messages that are sent come from anonymous accounts, while it is said that around 70 per cent comes from overseas. There is speculation that it comes from 'Russian or Chinese trolls', meaning agents of hostile foreign powers, with academic Savvas Zannettou quoted in *the New Statesman* saying,

> 'It will be totally unsurprising if trolls started sharing bad stuff for these players, given that their goal is to sow public discord, and this is an excellent opportunity to do so'.[190]

Then came reports of the racist vandalising of a mural of Marcus Rashford, who is lionised by many not just for his accomplishments in football, but also for his charity-work and political advocacy. Hundreds reportedly gathered by the mural, raising their clenched fists, 'taking the knee' and decrying racism, replete with conveniently-to-hand Socialist Workers' Party placards. £30,000 was raised to restore the image.

That the vandalism was racist was reported in *The Mirror, The Guardian, Manchester Evening News*, and on the BBC and ITV, and even made its way into *The New York Times*.[191] It was reported to the police as 'racially aggravated damage'; it will be recorded as a 'race hate crime' and will persist in police records as such, despite the fact there is no evidence of racial motivation. As pointed out by the journalist Brendan O'Neill, the graffiti said, 'F*** Saka, F*** Sancho. S***e in a bucket, bastard' – and with 'badly drawn' male genitalia pointing to Rashford's mouth.[192] It was not racist at all.

All the journalists had to do was to check what the graffiti said, which should have been a detail naturally to be reported to an audience that deserved to know the truth. It is worthwhile questioning the motivations of the media in this light. Why do they talk up to such an extent what are a tiny proportion of online posts made by people of no standing or significance whatsoever?

Much of the condemnation is accompanied by demands for regulation of social media companies, making it impossible to register accounts anonymously, as well as sanctions, including criminal penalties for senior executives. While these may seem appealing, there are many people who have an interest in seeing social media fail since it is beating the traditional media in the market for advertising revenues while profiting from their content.

Over the course of the 2020/21 season, the number of abusive posts was proportionally tiny. A study conducted on behalf of the Professional Footballers' Association (PFA) found of 6.1 million posts pertaining to football, 1,782 were deemed 'discriminatory'. That is 0.03 per cent. Half of the accounts responsible were located abroad, meaning 837 accounts from people living here. One third were 'homophobic', while 23 per cent were racist.

Such abuse is never aimed at gay players, since there are very few openly so. Rather, some may use such slurs when they perceive a player to have not given sufficient effort, to have behaved in an unmanly fashion, or have less ability. Moreover, the PFA study shows that such abuse peaked in December 2020, to coincide with players wearing rainbow-coloured laces to campaign against this. There is a very real possibility that they simply put into the minds of the crowd that this could be done. The same study found that of 650,000 social media posts sent after the Euro 2020 final,

324 were 'abusive' – or 0.05 per cent.[193] 'Toxic and racist safe space' hardly seems appropriate.

Critics such as Brendan O'Neill maintain that this is a moral panic, meaning we overreact to what is a problem, to the point that it becomes something akin to a mania. In the rush to be seen to be virtuous, we lose sense of proportion. If the fallout from the Euro final was for the English to lose their sense of accomplishment and instead turn on each other, all over a few hundred tweets that would, if left alone, have gone undetected amidst the millions of others, then it is safe to say O'Neill has a point.[194]

The inevitable consequence of this is that we fail to prioritise things correctly, with the resources devoted ultimately to protecting the feelings of very wealthy young men, being possibly better spent elsewhere. The BBC, for instance, incorporates the slogan 'Hate won't win' in its sports coverage, campaigning to end online abuse. Yet there are 600 murders each and every year. Can we not campaign to end murder? As shown in Chapter 3, the black murder rate is substantially higher. Ultimately, there comes a point where fashionable causes detract resources away from where they are most needed, namely to protect the lives of poor young black men, not the feelings of rich young black men.

As pointed out by Alex Krasodomski-Jones of the think tank Demos,

> 'Difficult subjects are often only accessible to some through anonymous communications: mental health, experience of end of life, sexual and gender identity and so on…
>
> 'Protecting the right to anonymity shows we care about an open internet in the face of authoritarian regimes' attempts to censor and suppress speech. And at home, anonymity is vital if we're going to protect leakers, whistle-blowers and investigative journalism and its sources.'[195]

Instead, he recommends better design of these websites, including restrictions on the ability of anonymous accounts to message, as well as 'reputation systems' that incentivise decency.

Forcing Twitter to edit in real time 350,000 'tweets' per minute would be the end of it. These companies exist on the proviso that they are not responsible for what is posted, only increasingly they are beginning to behave like editors.

The furore that followed has only served to make it obvious as to the gains that can be won for malicious actors – you can turn what ought to have been a moment of national pride, if not quite the victory hoped for, into one of shame and accusation – and that the costs are only born by other people, so long as you do it anonymously. Whether these people really are spooks or just nitwit malcontents is neither here nor there. The point is that in losing our sense of proportion, we increase the incentives for posting racial abuse, and only make likely more of it.

'Taking the knee'

Soon the rancour turned political, after England footballer Tyrone Mings took issue with Home Secretary Priti Patel condemning the racist abuse. Patel wrote on Twitter that she was 'disgusted' by the 'vile racist abuse' directed on social media to the England players. In response Mings wrote,

> 'You don't get to stoke the fire at the beginning of the tournament by labelling our anti-racism message as 'Gesture Politics' & then pretend to be disgusted when the very thing we're campaigning against, happens.'[196]

His post was 'liked' over half a million times.

Mings was referring to the 'taking the knee' which the English players performed before each of their matches in the European championships and has been performed by Premier League players before games since the death of George Floyd. Players had begun to 'take the knee', meaning to go down on one knee to symbolise their support for Floyd as well as their disavowal of racism, at a time when the grounds were empty due to Covid-19 restrictions.

It has also been associated to a large degree both with the sentiment and the movement of 'Black Lives Matter'. As the fans began to return, sections would boo, including at Colchester, Millwall, West Ham, and at England national games. Booing has also taken place at games in the United States. Patel refused to condemn the booing, labelling taking the knee as 'gesture politics'.[197]

In defence of Patel, it should be pointed out that she is as entitled as anyone to disavow racial abuse, since she has been the target of it.[198] Secondly, when we speak of 'gesture politics', we use it to criticise politicians for throwing a few million pounds at a problem in order to appear to do something rather than take it seriously. It is a metaphor. 'Taking the knee' is *literally* a gesture – and a political one. Some may argue that it is not political but simply a statement of basic moral decency. That is fine. But if we are to say morality is separate from politics, then this leaves us on very poor ground indeed.

Footballers have been doing this for over a year now, while athletes in the United States have been doing it longer. It is obviously not sufficient to put an end to online racial abuse, given what happened after the final of the Euros. Footballers have been telling us not to be racist for as long as I have been interested in football. Recall Les Ferdinand and Eric Cantona's advert from the 1990s – 'What do you see? A black man? A Frenchman? Or a footballer?' Stars such as Gareth Bale and Cristiano Ronaldo featured recently in an advertisement where they said in their many different native tongues, 'No to racism'. But most people do not regard sporting protests as beneficial. Polling has shown that just 22 per cent of ethnic minority individuals think 'public campaigns and protests against racism' help race relations, including 30 per cent of black people.[199]

Such feeling has been behind the dissent of Wilfred Zaha and Les Ferdinand. Whatever curative impacts the gesture might have had initially, we must also consider that they might wane with time, namely the phenomenon of *regression to the mean*. Ask yourself the extent to which standing on one leg before a match might bring about an end to terrorism, and you will see what I am driving at. English players had been kneeling before games for over a year, yet still it was not sufficient to stop racial abuse, something Mings failed to recognise.

In football it is anti-racism every week, but there are double standards. When Mesut Ozil spoke out against the persecution of Uighur Muslims by the Chinese government, his club at the time, Arsenal, declared itself 'always apolitical'.[200] As Ozil put it:

> 'There are a lot of black players and fans of Arsenal and it's fantastic the club is backing them.
>
> 'But I wish people would have done the same for the Muslims because Arsenal have many Muslim players and fans as well, and it is important for the world to say that Muslim Lives Matter.'[201]

The premier league has significant financial interests in China. The Chinese government responded to Ozil's protest by cancelling the broadcast of an Arsenal match against Manchester City – one of the biggest games of the season.[202]

Why does the sight of people kneeling down arouse such passions? Polling conducted by *YouGov* showed that football fans are fairly evenly split, with 49 per cent approve of 'taking the knee' compared to 41 per cent disapproving, with the caveat being that the question asked, stipulated that this was in 'solidarity with the Black Lives Matter movement'. Such wording may sway responses since this is a controversial political movement, regardless of the sentiments of the slogan. Support is strongest among younger generations, while middle-class fans are more likely to back it than working-class ones (56 per cent versus 39 per cent).[203] Note that 'fans' is defined by regular match-goers and TV viewers, and I suspect that among the former, disapproval would be most pronounced.

Consider the following extracts from an article by *The Guardian*'s football columnist, Barney Ronay, on booing at Millwall:

> 'To boo across the top is an act of violent disrespect totally out of kilter with the gesture itself, a handshake met with a punch to the throat…
>
> 'There doesn't seem much point at this stage in dwelling on the extraordinary lack of respect shown toward those for whom such gestures have a deep and personal meaning. Or on the inability to remain silent for five seconds if your politics preclude you from sharing the moment.
>
> 'Not to mention the fact that those involved must realise that booing – not ignoring, but actually p****** all over – a gesture that expresses anti-racism is by its nature a racist act.'

The article is vitriolic and concludes that the way forward is for all fans and the club itself to join together to 'punch up' by delivering a 'f***-you' to those in power, meaning, presumably, the Conservative government.[204] Ronay speaks to that tradition that believes saying 'f***' is a political act of great importance. The flaw in his argument is that the following week, the same fans cheered a banner unfurled by the same players that decried racism. Therefore, it must be something about going down on one knee that offends. But why?

Sam Ashworth-Hayes, writing in *The Spectator Australia*, makes the argument that it is because the gesture is associated with the political movement known as Black Lives Matter, which has been linked to Marxism, calls to defund the police, rioting, and rather than merely the sentiment expressed in the slogan:

> ''Taking a knee' is imported from America, tied to an American movement, arising from an American social context and tied to a set of demands alien to this country and its history…
>
> 'If a gesture or symbol is associated primarily with one cause, using it for a related one will mean people suspect that you are at best sympathetic to the original idea, and at worst trying to smuggle in support for it.'[205]

These arguments ring true, but I suspect they are only part of the story. Certainly, I can think of no other form of supposed anti-racism messaging at a football match that has been met with anything worse than yawns. While Ronay's writing is vitriolic, his righteous indignation finds echo in Mings' condemnation of Patel and elsewhere. It is clear, they think a moral standard which they hold dear has been violated. But no effort is made to try to understand why people might boo. Instead, they are dismissed with insults as 'racists, boneheads and people without compassion'.[206]

In his book *The Righteous Mind*, Jonathan Haidt describes how liberals (or leftists to be more precise) draw on a different moral framework from conservatives. Liberals respond to the world politically, based on two moral 'foundations', namely care and fairness. They seek to protect others from harm and ensure equality. Conservatives care about these things too, but their moral palate is more sophisticated in that they have an additional three moral dimensions. Haidt uses the metaphor of music in that conservatives hear an additional three octaves, that liberals are deaf to.

Conservatives also have the moral foundations of loyalty, authority and sanctity. Loyalty pertains to the standing of your group, family or nation, authority to respect for tradition, while sanctity pertains to abhorrence for things one finds disgusting. Notably, conservative moral values are most pronounced among the working-class, irrespective of support for conservative political parties.

I suspect that the booing of the 'taking of the knee' stems from the symbolism that jars with the moral foundations of loyalty and sanctity. The gesture was invented by NFL quarterback Colin Kaepernick as a way to make a protest during the American national anthem. Previously, he had sat through it, but having received criticism that this was somehow disrespectful to veterans of the armed forces, he knelt instead.

As the work of Gabriella Elgenius shows, people attach near-sacredness to the idea of the nation and its symbols.[207] Refusal to take part in its rituals will thus be taken as a sign of disrespect. Kaepernick deliberately targeted the national anthem but adapted his protest from sitting to kneeling to make it appear as if he was acknowledging the sacred, the sacrifice of others in service of the nation, while also voicing his disquiet. Note that his kneeling has an object, the national anthem, which is kneeled before. Doing so at kick-off in a football (soccer) match has none, and for this reason can look bizarre. Contrast this with the Scottish team that 'took a stand' against racism, meaning they stood together before kick-off in order to hasten an end to racism. That is obviously ridiculous, yet kneeling down is taken as solemn and compulsory and not to be disrespected or denigrated.

Kaepernick incorporated into his protest a gesture that has its own symbolic language. Kneeling down symbolises shame, humiliation, submission, remorse, and also sometimes devotion. But arguably the first person to 'take a knee', or both knees to be precise, was German Chancellor Willy Brandt when he visited the site of the Warsaw Ghetto in 1970, and known as the *Kniefall von Warschau*. While his contrition and shame as a German were fully warranted, their symbolic expression in this manner jarred with many Germans nevertheless, with 48 per cent saying it was excessive.[208]

Applied to the national anthem or the national team, this takes on a whole new language of connotation that is independent of the intent. People read into it what they will, beyond the control of Kaepernick et al. – and many see something they do not like, that jars with ideas they hold sacred.

Whatever the intentions of the footballers involved, it is the fact that other people will read into the gesture their own interpretation. People who feel those conservative values of loyalty and sanctity do not like it. To them, it seems like you are saying the country is no good. Most of these people will not be racist, but among their number, you will find most racists. The idea that you are going to bring about improvements in other people's behaviour by kneeling down before a football match (and that the effectiveness of this intervention will not wane), when this very gesture antagonises many people, among whom you will find the minority you wish to improve morally, is naïve, to put it mildly.

In essence, those who support the gesture see this as 'taking a stand' in line with the moral values of care and fairness. Those opposed, like the Millwall fans who boo it but applaud an anti-racism banner, are sensible to these values but are also sensing something they do not like. It seems we are talking at cross-purposes, only writers and columnists, such as Ronay, make no effort to understand and resort to insults. Indeed, the standfirst of his article claims those who boo 'desecrate' the taking of the knee, as though this were a religious ceremony and not something knocked up on the hoof by a malcontent reserve quarterback. Commentators such as Ronay miss the point that others are taking the very same gesture as 'desecration' of something else, that goes deep.

The booing seems to have died down recently, with the success of the England team being seen as them having earned the right to make the gesture. But that does not mean there is concord between fans and players. There may be a better way that can satisfy both, but we have to be realistic. The belief in the possibility of zero racism expressed on social media, which seems to be the measure of success of the England players, is naïve, especially given the many other horrors that lurk in the darker recesses of the internet. Moreover, anyone who has ever been to a football match knows that individual fans will misbehave, but the crowd will mostly tell them to shut up. There is a code of self-regulation. Douglas Murray writes of the 'madness of crowds', but football crowds tend, in my experience, to have pretty sound judgement and reward effort and brilliance, not race or nationality.

Summary

The English managed to turn a moment of accomplishment, if not quite triumph, into one of recrimination. Football, which provides something for people to enjoy and unify behind, within towns and cities as well as nations, has been hijacked by identity politics. We have become adept at creating new gestures and rituals that provoke bitter misunderstanding. The national sport becomes one of finger-pointing and not our beloved game.

6.

Lessons from the classics

Introduction

This report concludes with a short essay on how we might think about our ever-increasing level of diversity, and how we might still retain something distinctly British. It draws on insights from the classical canon of sociology to show how they might be useful and where we can go wrong in attempting to explain statistical disparity between ethnic groups. It then addresses some of the assumptions behind radical and even conventional thought, arguing that they promise the perfect world, only detail is mysteriously not forthcoming, while demands for money and power are. The alternative is to view British institutions as precious things that can benefit all, precisely because they have nothing within written down that would be truly exclusive to anyone other than a citizen.

Two approaches

There are those who maintain disparity between groups is caused by white racism or the design of British institutions. This is the basic position of the dogmatic left, which Conservative politicians such as Theresa May have accepted. Then there are those who say, no, these are actually relationships not between race and any given outcome, but between other variables such as class and region. We must tailor government interventions with regard to these variables and not race. This is the approach of the Sewell report.

Both look to explain statistical relationships in relation to other variables, without reference to the choices of individuals, whose resources and perceptions may vary. Such ideas map onto an age-old division in how we might persist in a science of society – sociology – which I come to below.

But first, take for example an article written by Raghib Ali, who is an NHS consultant and was responsible in part for the epidemiological analysis of the Sewell report.

He writes:

> '... we need geographically-targeted policies and interventions based on need, not ethnicity (but which will actually help those ethnic groups who have the highest levels of poverty the most – including deprived Whites.) Because the greatest determinant of your life chances today is not the colour of your skin but the circumstances into which you are born – and we must tackle this enduring injustice of 'systemic classism' to create a fairer Britain for all.'[209]

The problem is that the circumstances of our births are largely the result of purposeful and freely chosen behaviour by our parents, although sometimes circumstances may conspire against us. It is not an accident that people end up in middle-class jobs, nor something 'the system' brings about. People have to do things to get or stay there. Moreover, Ali is finding a 'systemic classism' based on inequality of outcomes, while I doubt he would permit the same method to diagnose 'systemic racism'.

In Ali's article there is another article struggling to get out. He writes of the importance of education and how when his parents arrived in Britain, they faced 'open racial discrimination' but 'never encouraged us to view ourselves as victims and stressed that education and hard work were the keys to a better future'. He contradicts his own argument by noting that poor children from some ethnic groups tend to excel. He writes of how he was on free school meals as a kid, yet today he is a successful scientist at Oxford University. His circumstances growing up were arguably not the determinant of his life, but rather conditions which his parents had both endured and chosen, and from which he ultimately flourished. What counted for Ali was his very *protestant work ethic,* drummed into him by wise and ambitious parents.

Durkheim versus Weber

The two facets of Ali's article express two stands of thought in sociology, existent since its inception. *Positivism,* associated with Emile Durkheim (1858-1917), sought to explain 'social facts' – consistently recurring patterns of outcomes – with reference to other social facts. The other side, known as *verstehen* – meaning something akin to 'deep understanding' and pioneered by Max Weber (1864-1920) – saw social life as purposeful and sought to outline the reasons why individual people came to pursue courses of action.

In his *Rules of Sociological Method,* Durkheim posits the idea that of 'social facts' as the object of sociology. While we might see these as outcomes that can be measured statistically, in other words a statistical variable, there is more, in that Durkheim sees these as existing independently of individuals and as exerting coercive power over them. These ideas are perhaps inconsistent, but what is of relevance is Durkheim's injunctive that:

> 'The determining cause of a social fact must be sought among the antecedent social facts and not among the states of the individual consciousness.'[210]

Explanations for ethnic disparity that rely on either 'systemic racism' or 'family structure' may be seen as a continuation of this approach, in that they explain one variable by another. They flounder in that they do not say precisely how, for example, one child sees his parents break up and goes off the rails, while another does not.

Weber's method, *verstehen,* instead sought explanations grounded in the motivations of individuals. He proposed four *ideal types* of purposeful social action by which he could explain any chosen social behaviour.

They were:

I. Traditional social action – we do things because they are following the time-honoured examples of those around us.

II. Affective social action – we do things based on emotional need without concern for the material consequences.

III. Value-based rational social action – we do things because they chime with a conscious belief in its inherent value.

IV. Instrumental rational social action – we do things based on goals and a rational appraisal of the benefits of what the action might bring.[211]

The advantages of Weber's approach come to light if we consider family breakdown. A family may break down (or not even be formed) because that is the social norm in the area where people live (Weber I). It may be because people seek to satisfy their own individual desires and marriage gets in the way of this (Weber II). Or because the welfare state allows one to afford children without marriage (Weber IV).

We can then posit that the children of such arrangements suffer from insufficient parenting, which becomes a vicious cycle across generations, further enhancing the effects of social norms (Weber I). This results in ethnic disparity, whereby the ethnic group in which this behaviour is most pronounced fares worse in education, employment and criminality. Contrast this with the Durkheimian approach, that says this there is a link but provides nothing as to why family breakdown occurs or matters. It is causal, somehow.

The Weberian approach has the additional advantage in that solutions more readily come to light. For Durkheim, society was an entity independent of its sum of parts, namely individuals. The purpose was to identify what was wrong and propose correctives. His approach lends itself towards the elite-directed interventions favoured by Sewell. Without specifying the individual causes, however, these seem doomed to flounder, creating more powerful elites, less freedom, and more government waste.

This is not to say there is no role for elites, but rather that it can be chosen wisely and with regard to the capabilities of the individuals they hope to direct, as well as respect for them as free individuals.

Attributing the demise of the family, and the black family in particular, to freely chosen and self-destructive behaviour will often be dismissed as 'blaming the victim' – with the person responsible for saying this seen as morally bad. But in what way is a black person in Britain a victim that a Bangladeshi is not? Moreover, taking the approach that black people are only and ever victims of white people or impersonal 'social forces', seems to deny them the humanity that anti-racists always sought to affirm. While one may fail at one's own hand, at least one is human enough to do so.

Weber may help us combat family breakdown in that we can show that it was not the social norm for black families in Britain in the 1970s (Weber I). We can argue that there is inherent good in conventional family life (Weber III). We can reconsider the incentives around family life, such as the tax system, as well as make the argument that whatever short term gains there might be are offset by the damage done to children. Moreover, there are massive gains to be had in being a successful father in terms of personal reward, pride and status (Weber IV). Looking on, you see that how much demand there is from black Britons for status and recognition, which is perfectly fine, only too many are missing out on what is most readily available closer to home.

Ultimately, the Sewell report may have identified a key variable, but did not address the mindset that lay behind it. Recall that the black family was in much better health at a time when poverty was greater and racism was more common and less taboo. Considering the issue from a Weberian perspective opens up approaches to solving the problem that may be useful to the Children's Commissioner in her post-Sewell work. It also shows us that the appeal must be to the head and heart of individuals, and not about the state nurturing relationships between individuals who have no idea why they should stick together. This brings us back to John Boyega's speech; if only those Black Lives Matter idealists, who have it in for racist statues of individuals long dead, might go after errant fathers or drug dealers and takers instead, who blight Britons of all colours far more.

Where Durkheim comes in handy

With its emphasis on family breakdown as causal, the Sewell report can be situated in a line of thinking that can be traced back to Durkheim's interest in the concept of *anomie*. This lineage includes the so-called Moynihan report of 1965, the findings of which are broadly echoed in Sewell.

To give it is proper name, *The Negro Family: The Case for National Action* was written by sociologist Daniel Patrick Moynihan, on behalf of the American government. He would later become a Democrat senator. He argued that racial equality in America had come to mean equality of outcomes between black and white, only this would not occur due to the decline of the black family, which was contributing to a widening disparity.

He attributed this to the legacy of slavery, which had included the violent disruption of black families as men and women were traded as commodities. Matters were compounded by urbanisation, which if it 'occurs suddenly, drastically, in one or two generations, the effect is immensely disruptive of traditional patterns'.[212] His report generated similar levels of furore and vitriol as Sewell's did, nearly 60 years later.

For Moynihan, the family matters in that it provides stability as well as the formation of morals and moderation on our impulses. Its loss leaves children without boundaries to allow them to function responsibility. The results are poor education, high joblessness, crime and addiction, which become self-sustaining across generations. He advocated efforts to repair the damage done, 'to strengthen the Negro family so as to enable it to raise and support its members as do other families.'

Moynihan was criticised for 'blaming the victim', but in truth, what he was talking about was *social anomie*, meaning a lack of rules or normlessness. This concept was used by the ancient Greeks but is mostly associated with Durkheim.

For Durkheim, anomie was caused by an increasing division of labour and rapid social change, whereby the traditional moral order and norms was no longer obviously relevant but nothing had transpired to take its place. In the British context, we might think of its increasing ethnic diversity, multicultural relativism and rapid churn of immigration as mapping onto such things, along with the 'parallel lives' that define the many segregated communities we have. For Durkheim, without the absence of moral restraint imposed from others, the individual turns to himself as source of morality, producing an egotism that can never be truly satisfied. Life becomes about seeking gratification of needs that cannot be met, leading to a lack of respect for authority and all manner of social ills.[213]

Related to this is 'strain theory' – developed by Robert Merton in the 1950s. This idea is that destructive and criminal behaviour comes about when the aspirations are there but the means to achieve them are not.[214] We might look at the disproportionate number of black people caught up in crime and conclude Merton's form of anomie to be causal. But Pakistani and Bangladeshi people have similar levels of poverty, will be subject to the same levels of racism, yet do not go down this route to the same degree. The key difference is that the latter are more likely to subscribe to a religion, Islam, that is far less susceptible to moral relativism and demands stricter restrictions on behaviour.

There is also the possibility that by promoting the idea of structural racism, we create the perception of unfair closure that brings about the sort of anomie that Merton had in mind.

Such reasoning provides an explanation that matches the data on ethnic disparity far better than those notions of oppression and 'structural racism', while also serving to fill in the blanks between the variables identified by the Sewell report. In essence, certain individuals flounder because they have insufficient rules. The solution to the problem of anomie is for social elites to restate traditional norms, as well as foster a culture that is not elitist but tied into those sections where disaffection is greatest. The government must be more committed to defending British institutions as beneficial to all. It must face down the radical critics, and this must be led from the top.

Disparity in the classical sociological canon

From its inception, sociology has been concerned with disparity between groups. For Weber, the question of his *The Protestant Ethic and the Spirit of Capitalism* was why Protestants were more successful economically than Catholics. The answer was because the Calvinist doctrine of *predestination* compelled them to seek out evidence that they were of 'the elect' and preordained to go to heaven, manifesting itself in economic endeavour and frugality. Durkheim's *Suicide* sought to explain why Protestants are more likely to commit suicide than Catholics. The answer lay in differing levels of social integration, with Protestants having an individual relationship with God at the expense of community relations, which led to them being subject to less social control.

Such explanations are anathema to many sociologists today who would rather Weber had addressed himself in terms of *Protestant privilege,* while clearly the disparity observed by Durkheim must have been down to systemic anti-Protestantism. For Karl Marx, the key disparity in question was between economic groups, although he did give consideration to differences between Jews and Christians in his *On The Jewish Question*. Differences between economic groups were to be explained by one group – the bourgeoise – exploiting another – the proletariat. The remedy was to be found in revolution, with the former liquidated and a new classless society, of which Marx wrote next to nothing of, to come instead.

Today's radicals

It is in this tradition that today's radicals belong. While the Black Lives Matter political movement is derided by critics as 'Marxist', it is not doctrinaire. While many simply see the slogan as self-evident, both as a moral statement and as an acceptance that they are oppressed. Instead of merely class, radicals see race as well as other variables such as sex, sexuality and transgenderism. And while they tend not to advocate violent revolution (with some being truly violent) nor the liquidation of the dominant groups they deem oppressors, they accept the basic premise of differences between groups being explained by exploitation within an unjust system.

Like Marx, they have next to nothing to say about what this perfect world, this new system, would look like. Instead, the method seems to be more akin to the 'long march through the institutions', with more diversity and inclusion workers employed by corporations and the state to bring about equality of outcomes, equipped only with busted flushes like unconscious bias training, and by scolding whites through epistles which begin 'Dear white people'.[215]

Consider a pamphlet written by Sanjiv Lingayah called *It takes a system: The systemic nature of racism and pathways to systems change.*[216] It is published by an organisation called

Race on the Agenda. In the pamphlet, he seeks to both define and provide remedy for systemic racism – which is an 'almost mystical concept' that 'obscures as much as it reveals' when used in common parlance.

He defines systemic racism as:

> '... the condition where society's laws, institutional practices, customs and guiding ideas combine to harm racially minoritised people.'

He continues:

> 'Ultimately, the existence and extent of systemic racism is an empirical question, revealed by familiar and persistent patterns of racial disparities in a range of domains. And on this empirical basis, there should be no doubt that our society is systemically racist.'

Unequivocally, then, group disparity of outcomes is evidence of systemic racism, only we are not told which laws, which facets of institutional practices and so on matter. Instead, we are simply to replace them with something yet to be imagined but which can be found only by fully funding 'our most creative advocates, activists, community-builders, researchers, story tellers, facilitators, campaigners, [and] artists'. How these people have any competence in what has never been accomplished anywhere is not considered.

He advocates:

> '... accepting systemic racism implies a radical reshaping of how we organise every aspect of social and economic life – including how we assess worth and how we distribute resources.'

His work was funded by the charitable foundation Lankelly Chase, one of those that denounced the Sewell report in the letter alluded to in Chapter 1. Do the people who run this organisation not realise that when Lingayah writes this, he has in mind their 'resources' as much as anyone else's?

The inclusive nature of British institutions as they are

If I am arguing anything in this paper, it is that British institutions benefit those of an ethnic minority while racism may persist with or without them. Lingayah's argument rests on the inference from disparate outcomes between white and those not white. Mine rests on comparisons between the typical non-white individual in Britain and their counterpart in their countries of familial origin. The results of the comparison are compelling in terms of life expectancy, health, education and wealth – and that is before we even begin to consider things like regional stability, freedom of expression, conscience and so on. All these things are preconditioned on British institutions as they are, not what might be.

For Lingayah, where disparity is consistent across time, where 'systems consistently deliver negative outcomes for particular populations', then that is a sign of intention, a 'design choice'. But this is little more than the argument of 'intelligent design' deployed by creationists in their battle with Darwin. And as I have shown in Chapter 3, in terms of education and class, disparity is not consistent across time.

Most of the British constitution and its institutions predate the arrival of the country's ethnic minority groups *en masse*. It is a common complaint that they fail ethnic minority people because they were not designed with them in mind. This is wrong; the lack of design allows for their inclusion, since there was never anything written to exclude them. The only specific mentions of race in our law are purposely there to ensure inclusion, namely anti-discrimination law, hate crime law, and the Equality Act 2010.

The abolition of slavery was brought about from within the British parliamentary and legal system, not by revolution from without. In 1772, in the case of *Somerset vs. Stewart*, Lord Mansfield declared slavery was not found in common law or statute and therefore had no legal status. Consider the later case of Joseph Knight, a black slave who won his freedom in a Scottish court of law in 1777, which established the precedent that Scots law could not uphold the institution of slavery.[217] As made clear by Neil Oliver, Knight's motivation was to be a free man so that he might live with his Scottish wife and child.[218] This was a black man using the existing British institutions to realise his freedom and that of others like him.

David Lammy found juries to be fair in their judgements on ethnic minorities,[219] yet the institution itself can be traced back to Danish invaders.[220] Moreover, there were specific provisions against Jews in Magna Carta, only such institutional racism no longer holds and Jews flourish here.[221] Our institutions may have at times unsavoury roots, but that is not to say there is not merit in how they function today. All too often, we enjoy what we are not prepared to defend.

Status redistribution and the classical canon

Political orthodoxy can be defined as such: that we must achieve 'representation' in the elites of society, meaning all groups should be proportionately represented relative to their share of the country's population, and that the state should nurture specific group 'identities' rather than promote what it is we have in common.

'Representation', is though a misnomer, in that if a black man works as a lawyer, he is not representing black people, but representing his client. The correct noun is 'presence'; he is there doing his job. Use of the term encourages us to think of individuals as facets of groups rather than autonomous beings with unique character and their own opinions. The preoccupation only ever extends to the social elites, since no one is bothered that white people make up 93 per cent of roofers but 86 per cent of the population.[222]

That the focus is on either the social elites or on the things that are revered culturally is important. The political left has historically been defined by policies pertaining to the redistribution of wealth. Such polices have tended to go astray in that the state seldom had better knowledge to reallocate wealth without engendering waste, resentment and blunting incentives. Instead, it seems the political left, and with it many on the right, has settled on the redistribution of status.

This takes us back again to Weber, who saw social stratification as more sophisticated than Marx did, being divvied up in terms of status as well as class and power. To understand the radicals, you have to understand that they see the world through status symbols. If some white people are seen to be in positions of power and influence, or widely admired and revered, then that is seen as a boon to all whites and a painful penalty for everyone else. Status is a zero-sum game. That Durkheim, Marx and Weber form the basis for any undergraduate course in sociology is seen as rewarding whites, making them feel at home, while alienating black and brown. 'Why is my curriculum white?', is the popular refrain.

The revealing response is, why is the curriculum not British? The answer is because European intellectuals did more to establish sociology and you cannot engage in the subject without addressing their legacy. The radical response is to look frantically for alternatives to supplement the canon by fiat in order to bring about a parity in supposed group status. While W.E.B. Du Bois was an important scholar, he was of the generation that came after sociology's foundation and his influence was substantially less. There are few black or Asian people in the Western canon because there were few black or Asian people in Europe, at a particular point in time, where a self-selecting group of people worked out a certain set of ideas. The discovered and enforced parity that is the intention of 'decolonising the curriculum' is thus artificial, and in essence, a lie.

At the same time, while the classics of the natural sciences include Darwin, Newton, Einstein and Maxwell, their actual works are seldom read at university, yet contemporary research publications from *within* Britain will feature many non-white authors, often Asian. It is not a coincidence that many of the most prominent expert opinions on the pandemic have come from individuals of an ethnic minority.

In terms of identity, we are to 'diversify' the curriculum, to 'decolonise' it, without explicitly saying what that entails. It can mean either including texts by non-white authors or marking revered writers, who did so much to define the national character, as suddenly objects of suspicion. Nor can the British classical canon proportionately represent its ethnic groups, since their histories are so different.

To recreate a canon is not something easily done, since classics earn their place over generations, with each coming to view a text and reappraise it in part on novel terms, in part deference to its antecedents. It is not something easily imposed; doing so rapidly flows into the territory of Mao's Cultural Revolution, giving licence to every politically-minded philistine under the sun. Moreover, there are double standards whereby long-dead luminaries of the Scottish Enlightenment, such as Hume and Burns, become targets for 'cancellation', but Michel Foucault, who died in 1984 and has been accused posthumously of some terrible things, attracts little opprobrium from the same sorts of people.[223]

Consider the fate of the Art History A-level which was withdrawn in 2016 in England due to an inability to recruit 'sufficient experienced examiners to mark and award specialist topics'. The offered curriculum had been designed to be 'global' rather than 'being a history of Western art', and would have allowed 'students to focus on art from countries, periods and cultures most relevant to them', according to its advocates.[224] In essence, it collapsed under the weight of its own multiculturalism since not enough people had sufficient knowledge to mark the exams. The balkanisation inherent in the design proved fatal. Teachers were being asked to teach things they were ignorant of. Had they focused on Michelangelo et al., then art history would have been possible at school. Instead, nothing was offered to students because the curriculum designers thought they could teach them everything.

Moreover, children, regardless of ethnicity, need to know what it is they are inheriting within Britain so that they can appreciate why it mattered, how it shapes them, and why it is precious. We privilege the inoculation of group-specific 'culture' over British culture, without realising this only equips the young to live within groups. At the same time, we want more ethnic minority individuals in position of leadership. The multicultural education that seeks to teach black children to be black, Muslim children to be Muslim and so on, is not equipping them with the cultural knowhow, the British tradition, necessary to conduct themselves responsibly in positions of leadership within our institutions. In other words, as the inheritors and custodians of things that have proven good for them. The radical voice that demands 'systemic' change without any detail offered only encourages their destruction, and this is reckless and philistine.

As we become ever more diverse, perhaps our political establishment might unashamedly ask those who are of ethnic minorities to cherish our institutions, to conserve them, and to repair them. To make it clear that they, like the white majority, are custodians of them as well as beneficiaries. This is the way to achieve proper integration, proper success, not chasing after something that cannot exist or is yet to exist and never designed. Moreover, I am beginning to notice a pattern whereby new designs proposed by 'anti-racist' campaigners are actually the *latest* designs, made without acknowledgement of past failed designs. They treat us as though we were all born yesterday, that we are gullible, which we often are, but also that they have no track record on which they might be judged.

Our curriculum should teach a story of Britain that shows why these institutions allow us to flourish in a free society, where you can be what you will, and free from government, so that we might learn how precious they are. It is not about telling the story of every 'community' so that they feel 'included', but why 'mad, bad and dangerous to know' kings and queens and politicians with sometimes dodgy views created a legacy from which we all may benefit.

As shown in Chapter 3, the minority middle-class is growing healthily. Whatever impediments there are have not been sufficient to stymy this, and this is true even for groups such as black Caribbeans, for whom educational attainment has been low. In this light, it is not immediately clear how necessary further government intervention or regulation is.

At the same time, there is a malaise across the country, more pronounced in some sections of society than others.

There is no reason why this ought to be. Family breakdown and its associated maladies are common among black families but rare among Asian ones. In what way is the former oppressed in that the latter is not? Ultimately, what is required is a reappraisal of some cherished notions of the left, pertaining to family and the individual, who in this worldview, obtains meaning in life through self-expression and in political conflict with the wider society. But this is not living either well or responsibly. If the government is to play a role in this successfully, it will not be brought about by technocrats with a 'theory of change', but only with popular support for a compelling argument as to why these things really matter.

Notes

1 The Spectator, 21 August 2021.
2 Bhopal, K. (2018) *White Privilege: The Myth of a Post-Racial Society*, Bristol University Press.
3 https://mises.org/wire/why-marxist-organizations-blm-seek-dismantle-western-nuclear-family;
https://www.spectator.co.uk/article/revealed-what-black-lives-matter-really-stands-for;
https://blacklivesmatter.com/defundthepolice/
4 https://www.spiked-online.com/2017/09/11/lammy-review-the-myth-of-institutional-racism/
5 https://news.sky.com/story/boris-johnson-told-to-scrap-use-of-bame-label-as-critics-brand-it-unhelpful-and-redundant-12259929
6 https://www.prospectmagazine.co.uk/magazine/black-boys-victimhood-school
7 https://www.standard.co.uk/news/politics/munira-mirza-boris-johnson-racism-inquiry-labour-a4470076.html
8 https://order-order.com/2021/10/19/beis-report-net-zero-must-navigate-structural-inequalities-institutional-racism/
9 https://www.civitas.org.uk/publications/how-we-think-about-disparity/
10 https://www.spectator.co.uk/article/the-truth-about-noah-carl
11 https://www.standard.co.uk/news/politics/commission-on-race-and-ethnic-disparities-report-slavery-marsha-de-cordova-b927301.html
12 https://www.theguardian.com/commentisfree/2021/apr/02/Sewell-race-report-historical-young-people-britain
13 https://www.ohchr.org/EN/NewsEvents/Pages/DisplayNews.aspx?NewsID=27004
14 https://www.gov.uk/government/statistics/hate-crime-england-and-wales-2020-to-2021/hate-crime-england-and-wales-2020-to-2021
15 https://www.ohchr.org/EN/NewsEvents/Pages/DisplayNews.aspx?NewsID=27004

16 https://www.theguardian.com/commentisfree/2021/apr/07/Sewell-report-structural-racism-research
17 https://www.health.org.uk/publications/build-back-fairer-the-covid-19-marmot-review
18 https://onlinelibrary.wiley.com/doi/full/10.1111/1467-9566.13001
19 https://www.gov.uk/government/publications/Covid-19-review-of-disparities-in-risks-and-outcomes
20 https://www.theguardian.com/commentisfree/2021/apr/07/sewell-report-structural-racism-research
21 https://www.theguardian.com/world/2021/apr/01/commission-race-report-used-cherry-picked-data-uk-public-health-experts-say
22 https://blogs.bmj.com/bmj/2021/03/31/structural-racism-is-a-fundamental-cause-and-driver-of-ethnic-disparities-in-health/
23 https://www.gov.uk/government/publications/the-report-of-the-commission-on-race-and-ethnic-disparities-supporting-research/ethnic-disparities-in-the-major-causes-of-mortality-and-their-risk-factors-by-dr-raghib-ali-et-al#fn:3
24 https://blogs.lse.ac.uk/politicsandpolicy/Sewell-report-labour-market/
25 https://www.equalityhumanrights.com/sites/default/files/research-report-108-the-ethnicity-pay-gap.pdf
26 https://www.gov.uk/government/publications/the-report-of-the-commission-on-race-and-ethnic-disparities/employment-fairness-at-work-and-enterprise
27 https://www.theguardian.com/commentisfree/2021/apr/01/sewell-report-no-10-racism-protests
28 https://www.theguardian.com/commentisfree/2017/oct/13/theresa-may-race-disparity-audit
29 https://www.civitas.org.uk/content/files/Disparity.pdf
30 https://www.bitc.org.uk/news/leaders-ask-pm-for-mandatory-ethnicity-pay-gap-reporting/ : https://www.gov.uk/government/publications/race-in-the-workplace-the-mcgregor-smith-review
31 https://hansard.parliament.uk/Commons/2021-04-20/debates/1502466F-D06B-402A-B7C0-03452FFB1DA9/CommissionOnRaceAndEthnicDisparities?highlight=Sewell#contribution-F601F8A6-CB95-4504-A9E0-CF77A028B7B3
32 https://www.theguardian.com/world/2021/mar/26/uk-businesses-may-be-forced-to-reveal-ethnicity-pay-gap
33 https://youtu.be/IruFXyiC0TM?t=1753
34 https://www.msn.com/en-gb/news/other/diane-abbott-and-sadiq-khan-leads-left-wing-fury-at-racism-report/ar-BB1fadg6

35 *Ibid.*
36 https://www.spectator.co.uk/article/a-brief-history-of-lived-experience-
37 https://www.churchtimes.co.uk/articles/2021/9-april/news/uk/commission-s-report-on-race-sets-inappropriate-tone-says-archdeacon
38 https://policyexchange.org.uk/wp-content/uploads/2017/03/The-two-sides-of-diversity-2.pdf
39 https://www.oxfordreference.com/view/10.1093/oi/authority.20110803100109997
40 https://www.youtube.com/watch?v=sG9rX6Ifzhw
41 https://www.spectator.co.uk/article/a-brief-history-of-lived-experience-
42 Sensoy, Ö. & Di Angelo, R. (2017) *Is everyone really equal? Teachers' College Press* (p187, 210).
43 https://www.spectator.co.uk/article/tony-Sewell-s-race-report-critics-are-guilty-of-gaslighting
44 https://www.civitas.org.uk/publications/how-hate-crime-policy-is-undermining-our-law-and-society/
45 https://www.psychologytoday.com/us/basics/gaslighting
46 https://www.psychologytoday.com/us/blog/pura-vida/201803/gaslighting-dummies
47 https://www.dailymail.co.uk/news/article-8410963/Furious-Priti-Patel-hits-Labour-accuses-gaslighting-BLM.html
48 https://hansard.parliament.uk/Commons/2020-06-08/debates/212DD2A6-B810-4FDE-B3BD-1642F5BA1E86/PublicOrder?highlight=will%20not%20take%20lectures%20from%20other%20side#contribution-C9ADFF22-51B7-4151-91C6-ED6A4E88BCAB
49 https://www.theguardian.com/commentisfree/2021/mar/31/the-verdict-on-the-Sewell-report-into-racial-disparity
50 https://hansard.parliament.uk/Commons/2021-04-20/debates/1502466F-D06B-402A-B7C0-03452FFB1DA9/CommissionOnRaceAndEthnicDisparities?highlight=gaslighting#contribution-41BA14D6-0F21-4A0D-A474-3EF22AE64830
51 https://www.spectator.co.uk/article/the-abuse-i-and-my-fellow-commissioners-have-received-following-the-race-report-is-unsurprising
52 https://www.theguardian.com/world/2021/apr/04/race-report-boss-wanted-schools-to-teach-the-truth-about-modern-britain
53 https://www.aljazeera.com/news/2021/3/31/uk-race-report-says-system-not-rigged-against-minorities
54 https://www.bbc.co.uk/news/uk-56585538
55 *Ibid.*
56 https://inews.co.uk/news/uk/former-asian-senior-policewoman-says-nonsense-to-claim-institutional-racism-vanished-1052859

57 https://assets.publishing.service.gov.uk/government/uploads/system/uploads/attachment_data/file/277111/4262.pdf
58 Williams, J. (1985) *'Redefining institutional racism' in Ethnic and Racial Studies* Vol. 8 No.3.
59 Graebner, C. & Ghorbani, A. (2019) *'Defining institutions – a review and a synthesis'*. ICAE Working Paper Series, No.89.
60 https://www.gov.uk/government/publications/public-sector-equality-duty
61 Stijn Baert (2017) Hiring Discrimination: An overview of (almost) all correspondence experiments since 2005.
62 https://www.youtube.com/watch?v=IruFXyiC0TM
63 Stijn Baert (2017) op.cit.
64 https://www.gov.uk/government/publications/the-report-of-the-commission-on-race-and-ethnic-disparities
65 https://www.civitas.org.uk/content/files/Disparity.pdf
66 https://bylinetimes.com/2021/04/09/race-report-sewell-commission-couldnt-find-something-it-wasnt-looking-for/
67 https://threadreaderapp.com/thread/1378001701781839872.html
68 https://www.theguardian.com/commentisfree/2021/apr/04/yes-we-need-a-more-nuanced-debate-about-race-but-this-flawed-report-fails-to-deliver-it
69 https://bylinetimes.com/2021/04/09/race-report-Sewell-commission-couldnt-find-something-it-wasnt-looking-for/
70 https://www.gov.uk/government/publications/the-report-of-the-commission-on-race-and-ethnic-disparities
71 https://www.civitas.org.uk/content/files/Disparity.pdf
72 *Ibid.*
73 https://assets.publishing.service.gov.uk/government/uploads/system/uploads/attachment_data/file/881317/tackling-racial-disparity-cjs-2020.pdf
74 https://www.civitas.org.uk/content/files/Disparity.pdf
75 https://www.equalityhumanrights.com/en/publication-download/unconscious-bias-training-assessment-evidence-effectiveness
76 https://www.bma.org.uk/bma-media-centre/Sewell-report-ignores-well-documented-evidence-of-structural-racism-in-the-nhs-says-bma
77 https://www.nhsrho.org/
78 https://www.gov.uk/government/news/new-body-to-tackle-health-disparities-will-launch-1-october-co-headed-by-new-dcmo--2
79 https://www.bma.org.uk/bma-media-centre/Sewell-report-ignores-well-documented-evidence-of-structural-racism-in-the-nhs-says-bma
80 https://www.gov.uk/government/speeches/speech-by-the-chair-of-the-commission-on-race-and-ethnic-disparities-dr-tony-Sewell-cbe

81 https://assets.publishing.service.gov.uk/government/uploads/system/uploads/attachment_data/file/974507/20210331_-_SEWELL_Report_-_FINAL_-_Web_Accessible.pdf
82 https://www.ethnicity-facts-figures.service.gov.uk/uk-population-by-ethnicity/demographics/families-and-households/latest
83 https://www.ethnicity-facts-figures.service.gov.uk/health/social-care/adopted-and-looked-after-children/latest
84 Li, Yaojun & Heath, Anthony. (2010). Struggling onto the Ladder, Climbing the Rungs: Employment and Class Position of Minority Ethnic Groups in Britain. 10.1007/978-90-481-8750-8_6.
85 https://thecritic.co.uk/template-for-technocrats/
86 https://www.ons.gov.uk/peoplepopulationandcommunity/birthsdeathsandmarriages/families/adhocs/12947proportionofchildreninloneparentfamiliesbyethnicgroupenglandandwales2019 ; https://www.ethnicity-facts-figures.service.gov.uk/work-pay-and-benefits/benefits/state-support/latest
87 https://www.yorkshirepost.co.uk/read-this/ministers-reveal-ps500m-support-package-including-75-family-hubs-but-industry-leaders-say-its-not-enough-3430568
88 https://www.ethnicity-facts-figures.service.gov.uk/education-skills-and-training/11-to-16-years-old/pupil-progress-progress-8-between-ages-11-and-16-key-stage-2-to-key-stage-4/latest
89 https://www.ethnicity-facts-figures.service.gov.uk/education-skills-and-training/11-to-16-years-old/pupil-progress-progress-8-between-ages-11-and-16-key-stage-2-to-key-stage-4/latest
90 https://www.thesun.co.uk/tvandshowbiz/11780885/john-boyega-speech-black-lives-matter/
91 https://blog.candid.org/post/what-does-candids-grants-data-say-about-funding-for-racial-equity-in-the-united-states/
92 https://www.equallyours.org.uk/funders-for-race-equality-alliance-report-a-quantitative-analysis-of-the-emergency-funding-to-the-uk-black-and-minority-ethnic-voluntary-sector-during-Covid-19/?utm_source=Equally+Ours+Newsletter&utm_campaign=81cade8f6f-Newsletter+April+1+2021&utm_medium=email&utm_term=0_104ed5022f-81cade8f6f-58974093
93 https://web.archive.org/web/20210421101547/https://www.acf.org.uk/news/commission-on-race-and-ethnic-disparities-response-from-foundations-to-the-prime-minister
94 https://www.alliancemagazine.org/blog/the-true-takeaway-of-uks-race-report-is-the-anti-racism-work-that-remains-heres-what-funders-can-do/

95 https://www.ethnicity-facts-figures.service.gov.uk/education-skills-and-training/11-to-16-years-old/pupil-progress-progress-8-between-ages-11-and-16-key-stage-2-to-key-stage-4/latest
96 https://www.ethnicity-facts-figures.service.gov.uk/housing/housing-conditions/overcrowded-households/latest
97 https://www.npeu.ox.ac.uk/assets/downloads/mbrrace-uk/reports/MBRRACE-UK%20Maternal%20Report%202019%20-%20WEB%20VERSION.pdf
98 https://policyexchange.org.uk/wp-content/uploads/2016/12/PEXJ5037_Muslim_Communities_FINAL.pdf
99 https://www.runnymedetrust.org/cerd-2021
100 https://unherd.com/thepost/the-runnymede-trusts-deeply-flawed-race-report/
101 https://www.legislation.gov.uk/ukpga/2010/15/section/1
102 https://www.bbc.co.uk/news/uk-politics-11771302
103 https://www.gov.uk/government/speeches/theresa-mays-equality-strategy-speech
104 https://www.gov.uk/government/news/pm-announces-new-independent-organisation-to-tackle-deep-rooted-injustices-in-society
105 https://www.gov.uk/government/news/pm-announces-new-independent-organisation-to-tackle-deep-rooted-injustices-in-society
106 The study can be found here, although you may need to use Way Back Machine to get a copy of it, since it has been removed from the internet, so far as I know:
https://www.semanticscholar.org/paper/Profiling-Populations-Available-for-Stops-and-Miller/1005d76d353c62fcd4bf334cfd6068079f09b13d
107 https://www.spectator.co.uk/article/the-stop-and-search-race-myth
108 https://www.equalityhumanrights.com/en/our-research/reading-lists/race-reading-list
109 https://www.equalityhumanrights.com/sites/default/files/prejudice-unlawful-behaviour-anti-prejudice-projects-race-on-the-agenda.pdf
110 https://www.equalityhumanrights.com/en/our-work/news/open-letter-prime-minister-runnymede-trust-our-letter-dr-halima-begum
111 https://cst.org.uk/public/data/file/7/4/JPR.2017.Antisemitism%20in%20contemporary%20Great%20Britain.pdf
112 https://www.standard.co.uk/news/uk/uk-best-countries-black-person-kemi-badenoch-a4459751.html
113 https://www.ons.gov.uk/peoplepopulationandcommunity/populationandmigration/internationalmigration/datasets/populationoftheunitedkingdombycountryofbirthandnationality

114 https://www.ons.gov.uk/peoplepopulationandcommunity/populationandmigration/internationalmigration/datasets/ipsmainreasonformigrationbycountryoflastornextresidence
115 https://ourworldindata.org/grapher/life-expectancy-at-birth-total-years; http://www.integrationhub.net/module/society-integration-and-everyday-life/#life-expectancy-general-health-and-diet (figures adapted by taking the average of men and women within ethnic groups)
116 https://www.ethnicity-facts-figures.service.gov.uk/health/wellbeing/well-being-happiness-yesterday/latest
117 https://www.ipsos.com/sites/default/files/ct/news/documents/2020-10/global-happiness-2020-report.pdf
118 https://www.oecd.org/PISA/
119 https://www.oecd-ilibrary.org/docserver/28450521-en.pdf?expires=1625579446&id=id&accname=guest&checksum=C1009D5083DB00788201358D2AA0ABCF
120 Data were sourced from various FOI requests to the Department For Education, found via www.whatdotheyknow.com, for example https://www.whatdotheyknow.com/cy/request/pisa_2015_data_by_ethnicity#incoming-1657070; All scores are averages across data points, weighted by sample size.
121 https://en.wikipedia.org/wiki/Programme_for_International_Student_Assessment
122 'Good grades' is used to describe differing but comparable measures of attainment at GCSE level. Between 1991 and 2006, the measure used is the odds ratio relative to white pupils for a given minority group in the share getting 5 or more GCSEs at grades A* to C. Between 2004 and 2013, the measure used is the odds ratio relative to white British in the share getting 5 or more GCSEs at grades A* to C, including in English and maths. Between 2001 and 2019, the measure changes to odds ratios relative to white British in the shares getting C or above in English and maths.
The statistics are sourced from here:
https://assets.publishing.service.gov.uk/government/uploads/system/uploads/attachment_data/file/439867/RR439B-Ethnic_minorities_and_attainment_the_effects_of_poverty_annex.pdf.pdf;
and here:
https://www.gov.uk/government/statistics/key-stage-4-performance-2019-revised:
https://www.ethnicity-facts-figures.service.gov.uk/education-skills-and-training/11-to-16-years-old/a-to-c-in-english-and-maths-gcse-attainment-for-children-aged-14-to-16-key-stage-4/latest

123 Northern Ireland Statistics and Research Agency (NISRA), Office for National Statistics, Social Survey Division. (2021). Quarterly Labour Force Survey, October - December, 2020. [data collection]. 4th Edition. UK Data Service. SN: 8777, http://doi.org/10.5255/UKDA-SN-8777-5

124 Li, Yaojun & Heath, Anthony. (2010). Struggling onto the Ladder, Climbing the Rungs: Employment and Class Position of Minority Ethnic Groups in Britain. 10.1007/978-90-481-8750-8_6.

125 http://www.integrationhub.net/why-are-muslim-women-less-likely-to-work/

126 https://assets.publishing.service.gov.uk/government/uploads/system/uploads/attachment_data/file/767789/Civil_Service_Fast_Stream_Annual_Report_2017_-_2018.pdf;
https://www.gov.uk/government/publications/public-appointments-data-report-201819/public-appointments-data-report-201819

127 https://www.ethnicity-facts-figures.service.gov.uk/workforce-and-business/workforce-diversity/nhs-workforce/latest;
https://policyexchange.org.uk/wp-content/uploads/2016/11/PEXJ5011_Bittersweet_Success_1116_WEB.pdf

128 https://fra.europa.eu/en/publication/2019/being-black-eu-summary

129 ONS data: https://www.ons.gov.uk/peoplepopulationandcommunity/personalandhouseholdfinances/incomeandwealth/adhocs/11095individualwealthbyethnicitygreatbritainjuly2010tojune2016andapril2014tomarch2018;
Credit Suisse data sourced from:
https://en.wikipedia.org/wiki/List_of_countries_by_wealth_per_adult#cite_note-CS-2021-1-1

130 https://www.cream-migration.org/publ_uploads/CDP_22_13.pdf;
Note that it is recently claimed that non-EEA immigrants now make a net positive contribution, but this was achieved by redefining 'immigrant' from being based on country of birth to nationality, thus stripping out all those who were born overseas but have acquired British citizenship from the category of 'immigrant'. This is not entirely satisfactory, since taking citizenship does not make the fact that you have migrated from one country to another, disappear.
https://assets.publishing.service.gov.uk/government/uploads/system/uploads/attachment_data/file/861246/Oxford_Economics_-_Fiscal_Contribution_of_EU_Migrants.pdf

131 https://data.worldbank.org/indicator/SL.UEM.TOTL.ZS?view=chart

132 https://fra.europa.eu/en/publication/2019/being-black-eu-summary

133 https://www.civitas.org.uk/publications/how-hate-crime-policy-is-undermining-our-law-and-society/

134 *Ibid.*
135 https://policyexchange.org.uk/accentuating-the-negative-on-race/
136 https://cst.org.uk/public/data/file/7/4/JPR.2017.Antisemitism%20in%20contemporary%20Great%20Britain.pdf
137 https://www.civitas.org.uk/publications/how-hate-crime-policy-is-undermining-our-law-and-society/
138 https://www.opindia.com/2020/07/muslim-grooming-gangs-uk-victim-narrate-details-rape/
139 https://fra.europa.eu/sites/default/files/fra_uploads/fra-2018-being-black-in-the-eu_en.pdf
140 https://www.civitas.org.uk/content/files/Disparity.pdf
141 https://www.thecourier.co.uk/fp/news/dundee/2481478/discrimination-row-humza-yousaf-and-nadia-el-nakla-to-proceed-with-legal-action-against-broughty-ferry-nursery/
142 https://www.equalityhumanrights.com/en/our-work/news/pontins-owner-signs-legal-agreement-prevent-race-discrimination
143 https://www.civitas.org.uk/publications/in-response-to-the-home-affairs-select-committees-report-the-macpherson-report-twenty-two-years-on/
144 https://www.civitas.org.uk/content/files/HomeAffairs.pdf
145 https://www.civitas.org.uk/content/files/HomeAffairs.pdf
146 http://www.integrationhub.net/module/attitudes-and-identity/#fnref-15
147 https://www.scientificamerican.com/article/microaggressions-death-by-a-thousand-cuts/#
148 https://www.gov.uk/government/publications/the-report-of-the-commission-on-race-and-ethnic-disparities
149 https://ajp.psychiatryonline.org/doi/pdf/10.1176/appi.ajp.162.1.12
150 https://www.ethnicity-facts-figures.service.gov.uk/health/mental-health/adults-with-post-traumatic-stress-disorder-ptsd-in-the-month-prior-to-survey/latest
151 https://www.ethnicity-facts-figures.service.gov.uk/culture-and-community/community/feeling-of-belonging-to-britain/latest
152 https://www.ethnicity-facts-figures.service.gov.uk/culture-and-community/community/feeling-of-belonging-to-a-neighbourhood/latest
153 https://www.ethnicity-facts-figures.service.gov.uk/culture-and-community/community/feeling-of-community-integration/latest
154 https://www.gov.uk/government/publications/the-report-of-the-commission-on-race-and-ethnic-disparities/foreword-introduction-and-full-recommendations
155 https://policyexchange.org.uk/pxevents/the-sewell-report-next-steps/

156 Muttarak, R. (2014). *Generation, ethnic and religious diversity in friendship choice: Exploring interethnic close ties in Britain. Ethnic and Racial Studies* 37 (1) 71-98. 10.1080/01419870.2014.844844.
157 https://www.age-of-the-sage.org/psychology/intergroup_discrimination_tajfel.html#henri_tajfel_intergroup_discrimination
158 https://www.jta.org/2018/10/17/united-states/harvard-once-capped-the-number-of-jews-is-it-doing-the-same-thing-to-asians-now
159 https://archive.md/20140927012454/https://www.aamc.org/data/facts/applicantmatriculant/157998/mcat-gpa-grid-by-selected-race-ethnicity.html
160 https://www.civitas.org.uk/content/files/HomeAffairs.pdf
161 Bhopal, K. *Op. cit.*
162 https://www.ox.ac.uk/about/facts-and-figures/admissions-statistics/undergraduate-students/current/ethnicity
163 https://www.theguardian.com/education/2017/oct/19/oxford-accused-of-social-apartheid-as-colleges-admit-no-black-students
164 https://www.ox.ac.uk/about/facts-and-figures/admissions-statistics/undergraduate-students/current/ethnicity
165 Kumar, S., Sherman, L.W. & Strang, H. Racial Disparities in Homicide Victimisation Rates: How to Improve Transparency by the Office of National Statistics in England and Wales. Cambridge Journal of Evidence-Based Policing, 4, 178–186 (2020). https://doi.org/10.1007/s41887-020-00055-y
166 https://www.gov.uk/government/statistics/race-and-the-criminal-justice-system-statistics-2018
167 https://metro.co.uk/2019/08/20/man-stabbed-stranger-death-cigarette-jailed-23-years-10604034/
168 https://www.gov.uk/government/statistics/race-and-the-criminal-justice-system-statistics-2018
169 https://www.southwarknews.co.uk/news/man-stabbed-stranger-in-neck-after-row-over-cigarettes-murder-trial-told/
170 https://unherd.com/2021/09/gangs-are-menacing-london-hospitals/
171 https://data.worldbank.org/indicator/VC.IHR.PSRC.P5
172 http://www.education.ox.ac.uk/wp-content/uploads/2021/05/Strand_2021_Report-to-SEWELL.pdf
173 https://www.civitas.org.uk/content/files/Disparity.pdf
174 https://web.archive.org/web/20210417092928/https://www.freeruk.com/blogposts/how-helpful-is-the-governments-new-measure-of-poverty/
175 https://www.civitas.org.uk/content/files/Disparity.pdf
176 https://web.archive.org/web/20160708103457/https://www.lse.ac.uk/sociology/pdf/Working-Paper_Introducing-the-Class-Ceiling.pdf

177 University of Essex, Institute for Social and Economic Research. (2021). Understanding Society: Waves 1-10, 2009-2019 and Harmonised BHPS: Waves 1-18, 1991-2009. [data collection]. 13th Edition. UK Data Service. SN: 6614, http://doi.org/10.5255/UKDA-SN-6614-14.

178 https://explore-education-statistics.service.gov.uk/find-statistics/apprenticeships-and-traineeships/2020-21#dataBlock-64553230-5641-4598-80ed-9f389bc3f92e-charts

179 https://www.tes.com/news/exclusive-cable-calls-overhaul-nightmare-levy

180 https://www.ethnicity-facts-figures.service.gov.uk/education-skills-and-training/a-levels-apprenticeships-further-education/apprenticeship-starts/latest

181 https://civitas.org.uk/pdf/SocialMobilityJUNE2010.pdf

182 https://www.amazon.co.uk/Head-Hand-Heart-Intelligence-Over-Rewarded/dp/1982128445

183 https://www.huffingtonpost.co.uk/2014/03/22/unpaid-student-loans-funding-crisis_n_5012484.html

184 https://www.thesun.ie/sport/7280122/twitter-deletes-racist-posts-england-players/

185 https://www.dsayce.com/social-media/tweets-day/

186 https://uk.news.yahoo.com/police-investigating-racist-abuse-england-230100155.html?guccounter=1&guce_referrer=aHR0cHM6Ly9kdWNrZHVja2dvLmNvbS8&guce_referrer_sig=AQAAAFeMYzfNhe-oenz3iqmmCn71619OKdguIrUannnza5gJtXT7K_GRrCbo7Zszb9q8h6vA2KtNHzF4whsdypx0uVhcUGDtZnuabdu4fmsJ29sgsKaEaGn6ofpQ5HCQGHjkyhQRjOV5nQqjIUKI7L1xXLasr8HtQFHnbBevB7ISgbk7

187 https://www.dailymail.co.uk/news/article-9778835/Racist-morons-bombard-Saka-Rashford-Sancho-abhorrent-abuse-trio-missed-penalties.html

188 https://metro.co.uk/2021/07/16/coach-arrested-for-racist-tweet-to-rashford-admits-he-may-have-sent-it-drunk-14937768/

189 https://www.spiked-online.com/2021/07/21/we-need-to-put-those-racist-tweets-in-perspective/

190 https://www.newstatesman.com/science-tech/social-media/2021/07/who-behind-online-abuse-black-england-players-and-how-can-we-stop

191 https://www.spectator.co.uk/article/the-marcus-rashford-mural-an-anatomy-of-a-moral-panic

192 https://www.spiked-online.com/2021/07/16/marcus-rashford-and-the-hysteria-about-racism/

193 https://www.thepfa.com/news/2021/8/4/online-abuse-ai-research-study-season-2020-21

194 https://www.spiked-online.com/2021/08/05/there-was-no-outburst-of-racism-after-the-euro-final/
195 https://twitter.com/akrasodomski/status/1414902136232624139
196 https://twitter.com/OfficialTM_3/status/1414655312074784785
197 https://www.bbc.co.uk/news/uk-politics-57778668
198 https://hansard.parliament.uk/Commons/2020-06-08/debates/212DD2A6-B810-4FDE-B3BD-1642F5BA1E86/PublicOrder?highlight=paki#contribution-C9ADFF22-51B7-4151-91C6-ED6A4E88BCAB
199 https://www.ncpolitics.uk/wp-content/uploads/sites/5/2021/03/bf-bme-1.pdf
200 https://www.bbc.co.uk/newsround/50811487
201 https://www.mirror.co.uk/sport/football/news/mesut-ozil-brands-arsenal-hypocrites-22516610
202 https://www.bbc.co.uk/newsround/50811487
203 https://docs.cdn.yougov.com/7xbmk8cm3y/YouGov%20-%20EPL%20Kneeling%20Results.pdf
204 https://www.theguardian.com/football/2020/dec/07/taking-a-knee-is-a-sign-to-minorities-they-are-welcome-at-football-grounds
205 https://spectator.com.au/2021/06/what-the-england-team-doesnt-get-about-taking-the-knee/
206 https://www.theguardian.com/football/blog/2021/jun/06/england-fans-booing-taking-knee-euro-2020
207 Elgenius, G. (2019) Symbols of nations and nationalism: celebrating nationhood. Palgrave Macmillan.
208 https://en.wikipedia.org/wiki/Kniefall_von_Warschau
209 https://www.conservativehome.com/platform/2021/07/raghib-ali-systemic-classism-not-racism-wny-the-main-factor-in-health-and-educational-inequalities-is-deprivation-not-race.html
210 Durkheim, Émile. [1895] 2004. "The Rules of Sociological Method." Pp. 43–63 in *Readings from Emile Durkheim*. Rev. ed., edited and translated by K. Thompson. New York: Routledge; quoted here: https://sociologydictionary.org/social-fact/
211 https://revisesociology.com/2017/01/26/max-webers-social-action-theory/
212 https://web.stanford.edu/~mrosenfe/Moynihan%27s%20The%20Negro%20Family.pdf
213 https://faculty.rsu.edu/users/f/felwell/www/Theorists/Essays/Durkheim1.htm
214 https://www.simplypsychology.org/mertons-strain-theory-deviance.html
215 https://senioronboarding.leadershipacademy.nhs.uk/blog-dear-white-people-in-the-uk/
216 https://www.rota.org.uk/publications/systemsreport2021

217 https://en.wikipedia.org/wiki/Joseph_Knight_(slave)#Appeal_to_the_Court_of_Session

218 Oliver, N. (2010) *A History of Scotland*. Weidenfeld & Nicholson; http://www.metnews.com/articles/2015/perspectives072015.htm

219 https://www.gov.uk/government/organisations/lammy-review

220 https://www.gov.uk/government/publications/lammy-review-final-report;

221 https://www.thejc.com/magna-carta-s-three-jewish-clauses-1.56652

222 https://policyexchange.org.uk/wp-content/uploads/2017/03/The-two-sides-of-diversity-2.pdf

223 https://thecritic.co.uk/issues/april-2021/michel-foucault-the-prophet-of-pederasty/

224 https://www.bbc.co.uk/news/education-37642722

CIVITAS

Our Aims and Programmes

- We facilitate informed public debate by providing accurate factual information on the social issues of the day, publishing informed comment and analysis, and bringing together leading protagonists in open discussion. Civitas never takes a corporate view on any of the issues tackled during the course of this work. Our current focus is on issues such as education, health, crime, social security, manufacturing, the abuse of human rights law, and the European Union.

- We ensure that there is strong evidence for all our conclusions and present the evidence in a balanced and objective way. Our publications are usually refereed by independent commentators, who may be academics or experts in their field.

- We strive to benefit public debate through independent research, reasoned argument, lucid explanation and open discussion. We stand apart from party politics and transitory intellectual fashions.

- Uniquely among think tanks, we play an active, practical part in rebuilding civil society by running schools on Saturdays and after-school hours so that children who are falling behind at school can achieve their full potential.

Subscriptions and Membership (UK only)

If you would like to stay abreast of Civitas' latest work, you can have all of our books delivered to your door as soon as they are published. New subscribers receive a free copy of Roger Bootle's book, *The AI Economy: Work, Wealth and Welfare in the Robot Age* and Daniel Bentley's book, *The Land Question* on fixing the dysfunction at the root of the housing crisis. For those who would like to support our work further and get involved in our Westminster events, we have a variety of Subscription and Membership options available:
https://www.civitasonline.org.uk/product-category/subscriptions/

We regret that we are unable to post items to non-UK residents, although all of our publications are individually available via our Civitas Book Store (https://www.civitasonline.org.uk) and in most cases on Amazon.

Renewals for Existing Members

If you are an existing member wishing to renew with ease and convenience, please do select one of the subscription or membership options that most closely meets your requirements.

Make a Donation

If you like our work and would like to help see it continue, please consider making a donation. A contribution of any amount, big or small, will help us advance our research and educational activities. You can make a donation by getting in touch (020 7799 6677) or sending a simple email to info@civitas.org.uk so that we can come back to you.

Supporters of Civitas

Because we want to reach as wide an audience as possible, our subscription and membership fees are set as low as possible and barely meet printing and postage expenses. To meet the costs of producing our research and conducting our educational projects, we rely entirely on the goodwill and generosity of people who value our work.

If you would like to support our work on a rolling basis, there is a variety of advanced membership levels on offer. Supporters of Civitas have the opportunity to become more deeply engaged with the work their philanthropy makes possible.

You can pay by selecting a membership or subscription option and we will be in contact.

Alternatively, just call us on +44 (0)20 7799 6688
or email info@civitas.org.uk and we can discuss your options.

If it is your preference, please make cheques payable to Civitas.

Civitas: Institute For The Study Of Civil Society
First Floor
55 Tufton Street
Westminster
London
SW1P 3QL

Email: subs@civitas.org.uk

Civitas is a registered charity, No. 1085494